INTRODUCING

Consciousness

David Papineau and Howard Selina

Edited by Richard Appignanesi

ICON BOOKS UK TOTEM BOOKS USA

Published in the United Kingdom in 2000 by Icon Books Ltd., Grange Road, Duxford, Cambridge CB2 4QF email: icon@mistral.co.uk www.iconbooks.co.uk

Distributed in the UK, Europe, Canada, South Africa and Asia by the Penguin Group: Penguin Books Ltd., 27 Wrights Lane, London W8 5TZ

Published in Australia in 2000 by Allen & Unwin Pty. Ltd., PO Box 8500, 9 Atchison Street, St. Leonards NSW 2065

Published in the United States in 2000 by Totem Books Inquiries to: PO Box 223, Canal Street Station, New York, NY 10013

In the United States, distributed to the trade by National Book Network Inc., 4720 Boston Way, Lanham, Maryland 20706

Library of Congress Catalog Card Number: 99–085703

ISBN 1 84046 115 2

Originating editor: Richard Appignanesi

Printed and bound in the UK by
Biddles Ltd., Guildford and King's Lynn

What is Consciousness?

The best way to begin is with examples rather than definitions.

Imagine the difference between having a tooth drilled without a local anaesthetic...

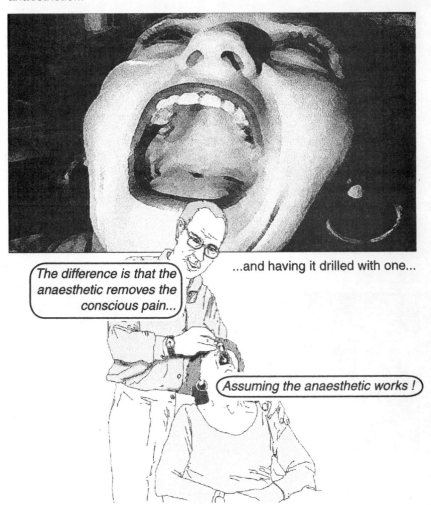

...and having it drilled with one...

The difference is that the anaesthetic removes the conscious pain...

Assuming the anaesthetic works !

Again, think of the difference between having your eyes open and having them shut...
When you shut your eyes, what disappears is your conscious visual experience.

Sometimes consciousness is explained as the difference between being awake and being asleep. But this is not quite right.

Dreams are sequences of conscious experiences, even if these experiences are normally less coherent than waking experiences.

Indeed, dream experiences, especially in nightmares or fantasies, can consciously be very intense, despite their lack of coherence – or sometimes because of this lack.

Consciousness is what we lose when we fall into a **dreamless** sleep or undergo a total anaesthetic.

The Indefinability of Consciousness

The reason for starting with examples rather than definitions is that no objective, scientific definition seems able to capture the essence of consciousness.

For example, suppose we try to define consciousness in terms of some characteristic **psychological** role that all conscious states play – in influencing decisions, perhaps, or in conveying information about our surroundings.

Or we might try to pick out conscious states directly in **physical** terms, as involving the presence of certain kinds of chemicals in the brain, say.

Any such attempted objective definition seems to leave out the essential ingredient. Such definitions fail to explain why conscious states **feel** a certain way.

Couldn't we in principle build a robot which satisfied any such scientific definition, but which had no real feelings?

Imagine a computer-brained robot whose internal states register "information" about the world and influence the robot's "decisions". Such design specifications alone don't seem to guarantee that the robot will have any real feelings.

The lights may be on, but is anyone at home?

The same point applies even if we specify precise chemical and physical ingredients for making the robot.

Why should an android become conscious, just because it is made of one kind of material rather than another?

There is something ineffable about the felt nature of consciousness. We can point to this subjective element with the help of examples. But it seems to escape any attempt at objective definition.

Louis Armstrong (some say it was Fats Waller) was once asked to define jazz.

What is it Like to be a Bat?

When we talk about conscious mental states, like pains, or visual experiences, or dreams, we often run together subjective and objective conceptions of these states. We don't stop to specify whether we mean to be talking about the **subjective feelings** – what it is *like* to have the experience – or the **objective features** of psychological role and physical make-up.

Even so, these two sides can always be distinguished. This is the point of the American philosopher Thomas Nagel's famous question: "What is it like to be a bat?"

Most bats find their way about by echo-location. They emit bursts of high-pitched sound and use the echoes to figure out the location of physical objects. So the intent of Nagel's question is: "What is it like for bats to sense objects by echo-location?"

It must be like living in the dark, spending a lot of time hanging upside down, and hearing a barrage of high-pitched noises.

But this is unlikely.

That's perhaps what it would be like for humans to live as bats do.

But for bats, to whom echo-location comes naturally, it is presumably not sounds they are aware of, but physical objects – just as vision makes humans aware of physical objects, not light waves.

But still, what is it like for bats to sense physical objects? Do they sense them as being bright or dark or coloured? Or do they rather sense them as having some kind of sonic texture? Do they even sense shapes as we do?

We can't answer these questions. We don't have a clue about what it is like to be a bat.

In raising his question, Nagel does not want to suggest that bats lack consciousness. He takes bats to be normal mammals, and as such just as likely to be conscious as cats and dogs. Rather, he wants to force us to distinguish between the two conceptions of conscious experiences, **objective** and **subjective**.

When we think about humans, we don't normally bother about Nagel's distinction. We usually think of human consciousness simultaneously in subjective and objective terms – both in terms of how it feels and in terms of objectively identifiable goings-on in the brain.

The bats, however, force us to notice the distinction, precisely because we don't have any subjective grasp of bat sensations, despite having plenty of objective information about them.

Science tells us a great deal about the bat's brain.

But not what it is like to be a bat.

Experience and Scientific Description

Nagel thus identifies something about experience that escapes scientific description. We lack this subjective something with bats, even after knowing everything science can tell us about them.

The moral then applies to conscious experiences in general.

How Does Consciousness Fit In?

The central problem of consciousness relates to mental states with a subjective aspect. In Nagel's words, these are states that are "like something". They are also sometimes called **phenomenally** conscious to emphasize their distinctive "what-its-likeness".

The big challenge is to explain how subjective or phenomenal consciousness fits into the objective world.

And in particular how it relates to scientific goings-on in the brain.

We face a number of choices at this point. Let's look at the three options that will emerge: **dualist**, **materialist** and **mysterian**.

The First Option: Dualist

Are the subjective features of conscious experience genuinely **distinct** from brain activities? This is a natural assumption. But this is a **dualist** line which then raises further questions.

*If the world contains subjective elements, then how do they **interact** with the normal physical entities which seem to fill up space and time?*

And what yet unknown principles govern the emergence of these subjective elements?

The Second Option: Materialist

An alternative is to deny that subjective mind and objective brain are as distinct as they appear to be. This **materialist** option is suspicious of the divergence between subjective and objective conceptions of the mind-brain. It insists on a **unity** behind the appearances.

The Third Option: Mysterian

Yet others despair of the problem and settle for the "**mysterian**" view that consciousness is a complete mystery.

We will examine these options more closely later. For the moment let us simply agree, in the terminology of the Australian philosopher David Chalmers, that explaining phenomenal consciousness is the "**hard problem**" of consciousness.

Hard and Easy Problems

Chalmers distinguishes between the "hard problem" and "easy problems" of consciousness. According to Chalmers, the easy problems concern the objective study of the brain.

Of course, these problems are only "easy" in a relative sense. They can pose real challenges to psychologists and physiologists. But they are "easy" in seeming soluble by straightforward scientific methods, and not raising any insurmountable philosophical obstacles.

So, for example, we might analyse **pain** as a state that is typically caused by bodily damage, and which typically causes a desire to avoid further damage.

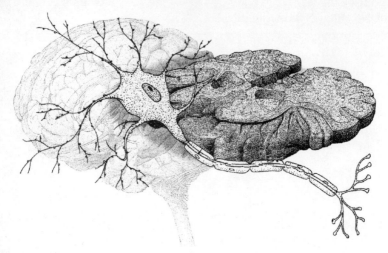

Then we can investigate how pain is realized in humans by a system of A-fibre and C-fibre transmissions, and by different physiological systems in other animals.

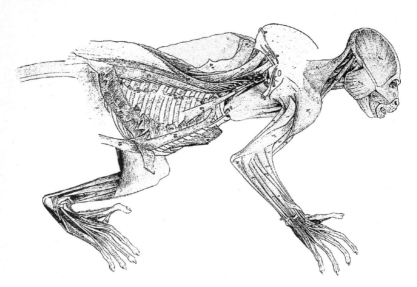

Similar objective studies can be carried out for other psychological processes like vision, hearing, memory, and so on.

But none of this "easy" stuff, Chalmers points out, tells us anything at all about the **feelings** involved. Stories about causal roles and physical realizations will apply just as much to unfeeling robots as to throbbing, excited, itching human beings. The "hard problem" is to explain **where** the feelings come from – to explain phenomenal consciousness.

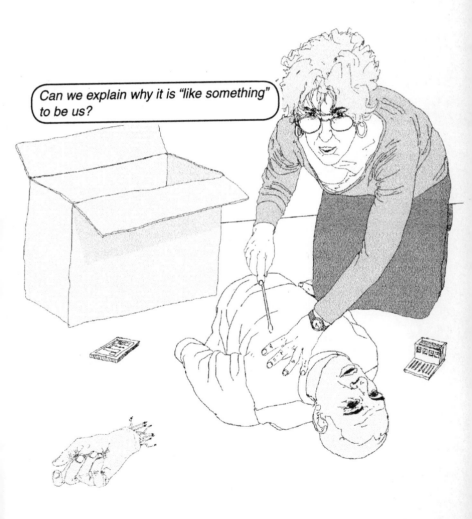

The Explanatory Gap

Another philosopher, the American Joseph Levine, calls this problem "the explanatory gap". Objective science can only take us so far. In psychology, as elsewhere, it can identify how different states function causally, and can figure out the mechanisms involved. But in psychology this doesn't seem to be enough. There is something else to explain.

Even after we have been told all about damage-avoiding states and A-fibres and C-fibres, we still want to say …

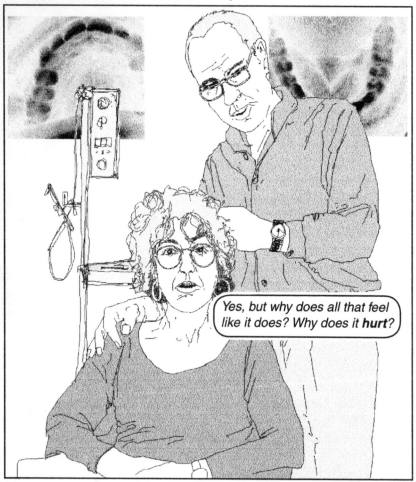

*Yes, but why does all that feel like it does? Why does it **hurt**?*

There seems to be a gap here between what science can tell us and what we most want to explain.

Creature Consciousness

Sometimes we speak of **creatures** being conscious, rather than of their having phenomenally conscious *states*. For example, we say that humans are conscious and bacteria are not. And we might wonder whether fish are conscious, say, or snails.

But talk of "creature consciousness" isn't significantly different from our earlier talk of phenomenally conscious states. "Creature consciousness" can easily be defined in terms of "state consciousness". A creature is conscious if it sometimes has conscious states.

Whether fish are conscious simply comes down to the question of whether they sometimes have conscious pains, conscious visual experiences, and so on.

The Hard Problem is New

The hard problem of consciousness has emerged into prominence in the second half of the 20th century. This is because the world-view developed by 20th-century science has made it hard to understand how consciousness can fit into reality.

The physical world, as conceived by contemporary science, threatens to squeeze consciousness out of existence.

*Once the world has been filled with **forces**, **atoms** and **molecules**...*

... there seems no room left for separate conscious states.

It has not always been so. Before the 20th century, both philosophers and scientists took it for granted that reality included independent conscious minds, separate from any material reality.

It was widely assumed that the conscious realm is at least as basic as the world of matter.

Historically, it was matter that was viewed as a second-class citizen, not mind.

René Descartes' Dualism

René Descartes (1596–1650) is widely regarded as the originator of modern philosophy. He also laid the foundations for modern physical science. But despite his innovatory ideas about the physical world, he never doubted that conscious minds exist on a separate, non-physical level.

Descartes was a dualist. He thought that there are two separate but interacting realms, the mental and the material.

Matter in Motion

Descartes' view of the material world was itself very austere, quite different from previous views, and indeed from much subsequent thinking. He assumed that the material realm contains nothing but matter in motion, and that all action is by contact.

All physical effects are caused by bits of matter bumping into each other.

Colours, sounds, smells and so on, are not really in the objects themselves, but are impressions produced in us by the action of material particles on our sense organs.

Mind Separate From Matter

Descartes did not take reality to be exhausted by matter in motion. In partial compensation for the austerity of his material world, Descartes also postulated a separate realm of mind. This other realm was populated by thoughts and emotions, pleasures and pains. These conscious elements had none of the **spatial** characteristics of matter – namely, size, shape and motion.

The only property they share with material events is that of being located in time.

Descartes took it that mind and matter could interact, despite their radical differences. Material causes can produce mental effects, as when you sit on a material pin and so feel a mental pain. And mental causes can produce material effects, as when your mental pain causes you to jump up again.

The Pineal Gland

Descartes thought that mind and matter interact in the **pineal gland**. This is a pea-sized organ in the human brain, situated beneath the corpus callosum, whose function is still not fully understood. It is also the only symmetrical organ in the brain without a left and right counterpart.

This is where material and mental events get together to affect each other.

This may now seem a wacky idea, but it was an honest answer to a serious problem. Any version of dualism needs somehow to explain how its two distinct realms – mind and matter – can interact causally. Later we shall see that this remains the Achilles' heel of contemporary dualist views. Descartes' pineal gland theory is often mocked, but some account of mind-brain interaction is a necessary part of any dualist view.

Berkeley's World of Ideas

The problem of mind-matter interaction continued to perturb Descartes' successors. They also worried about our ability to know about the material world.

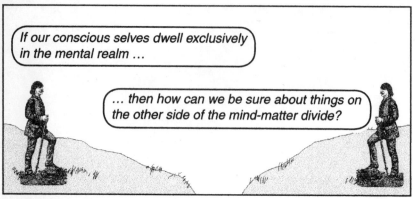

If our conscious selves dwell exclusively in the mental realm ...

... then how can we be sure about things on the other side of the mind-matter divide?

Sceptics argued that Descartes' dualism condemns us to ignorance about the world of matter.

George Berkeley (1685–1753), Bishop of Cloyne, proposed a radical solution to both these problems.

*Suppose there is **no material world** – just the world of mental events.*

That is, suppose that all our experiences are just as they are, but that there are no physical objects "out there" causing those experiences. Then everything would continue to appear as normal, even though there would be nothing in reality except mental experiences.

Berkeley's radical **idealism** has obvious attractions. There is no longer any problem of mind-matter interaction, since there is no matter left for mind to interact with.

Nor is there any problem about our knowledge of the "external world", since the external world has been abolished.

"Esse est percipi" said Berkeley – "To be is to be perceived" – and at a stroke he dissolved the problems facing Descartes' dualism.

Of course, idealism is an affront to common sense. It certainly outraged Berkeley's contemporary, the lexicographer and man of letters **Samuel Johnson** (1709–84). Johnson could not take Berkeley's denial of matter seriously.

Idealism cannot be dismissed so easily. Berkeley would of course allow that Johnson could *see* a stone and *feel* the pain as he kicked it. He would just deny that the cause of these subjective impressions is some supposed **further** material entity. And how could Johnson prove Berkeley wrong, given that his only evidence would be yet further subjective impressions?

The Idealist Tradition

This impregnability to disproof, plus its philosophical advantages, has attracted many philosophers to idealism.

Indeed, nearly every significant philosopher from the late 18th century to the early 20th century has been a paid-up idealist.

Among the most eminent have been the German philosophers **Georg Hegel** (1770–1831), **Arthur Schopenhauer** (1788–1860) and **Edmund Husserl** (1859–1938), and the French philosopher **Henri Bergson** (1859–1941).

Idealism in Britain

Nor should it be thought that idealism has been an exclusively Continental disease. British philosophy is renowned for its adherence to common sense, but that has not stopped its leading figures signing up to the idealist cause.

John Stuart Mill (1806–73) was in most respects an entirely sober mind, an advocate of systematic scientific research, who for many years worked as a pillar of the British East India Company. But about the nature of the material world he was a dedicated follower of Berkeley.

Stones, sticks and other physical things have no separate reality apart from our sensory awareness of them.

For Mill, material objects are "permanent possibilities of sensation".

This tradition of British idealism was continued by Mill's godson, **Bertrand Russell** (1872–1970). Russell was a great logician and philosopher of language.

The Berkeleyan tradition was carried even further into the 20th century by **A.J. Ayer** (1910–89). "Freddie" Ayer was the epitome of 20th-century urbanity, with a glamorous social life and frequent appearances on television. His wider public would probably have been surprised to know that he too thought that the material world has no reality apart from its reflection in the deliverances of our sense organs.

The Scientific Reaction to Idealism

Whatever you may think of idealism, you must admit that it doesn't have any problem with consciousness. Far from struggling to find a place for conscious states within reality, idealists build reality out of consciousness. Their problem is to explain how physical objects like trees and tables can be part of reality, not how consciousness can.

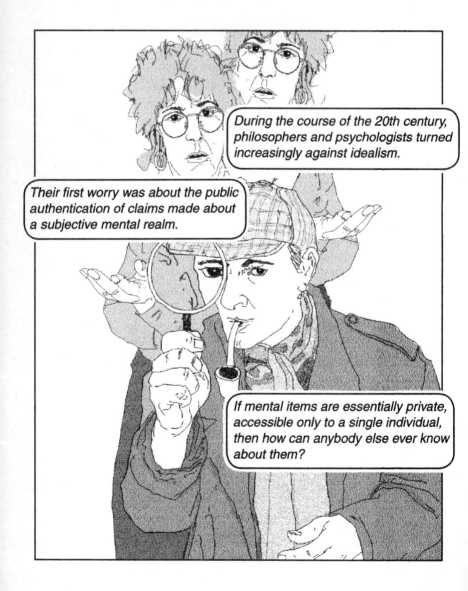

Behaviourist Psychology

This worry first surfaced within psychology. The **Behaviourist** movement argued that a scientific psychology cannot be built on introspection of subjective states. The pioneers of Behaviourism were **John B. Watson** (1878–1958) and, following him, **B.F. Skinner** (1904–90).

The Behaviourist school learned a great deal from experimental studies on rats and pigeons, and in particular about how they could be trained by appropriate patterns of reward and punishment.

The Skinner Box

Skinner designed a special experimental device, the "Operant Conditioning Apparatus", nicknamed the "Skinner Box", to study the conditioned reflex behaviour of rats. When a rat presses a lever in one wall of the box, a food reward is delivered through an aperture. The rat might press the lever by accident, at first, but the reward will **reinforce** it to continue pressing.

Skinner discovered that a rat, once reinforced, will continue to press the lever even if the food reward is stopped. It has been "operantly conditioned".

Both Watson and Skinner applied their views to humans, as well as to rats and pigeons. Watson was an extreme environmentalist.

*The structure of the human mind is shaped entirely by **nurture** – in the form of rewards and punishments – and not by **genetic nature.***

In line with this, Skinner wrote a widely-read utopian novel, *Walden Two*, as a sequel to **Henry Thoreau**'s (1817–62) original American rural idyll, in which he urged a system of child-raising built on rigorous patterns of reward.

The Ghost in the Machine

The Behaviourist movement in psychology received influential backing from philosophers. Where the psychologists rejected the study of subjective experiences as bad methodology, the philosophers argued that subjective experiences made no logical sense at all. This philosophical position became known as "logical behaviourism" to distinguish it from the weaker "methodological behaviourism" of the psychologists.

The logical behaviourists dismissed the notion of subjective individual experience as incoherent.

All we can seriously mean by talk of "mental states" are publicly observable inclinations to behave in certain ways.

Gilbert Ryle (1900–76) ridiculed the traditional picture of the mind as a separate subjective realm controlling the movements of the body. He called this picture "the ghost in the machine". He rejected it in favour of the view that mental attributes are simply dispositions to behave in certain ways.

The Beetle in the Box

Another philosopher associated with logical behaviourism was **Ludwig Wittgenstein** (1889–1951). In his famous "private language argument", Wittgenstein urged that public verification is essential to the workings of language. There is no sense to a language whose claims can be checked by only one person. Talk of mental states can't possibly refer to private inner episodes. If it did, we wouldn't know what we were talking about.

It would be as if we each had a box that no one else could look into, and all started talking about the "beetle" in our box.

We might all mean different things by "the beetle in the box" – or nothing at all.

If mental talk is to have any objective content, argued Wittgenstein, we must regard the mental realm as intrinsically connected to the behaviour which makes it publicly observable.

Psychological Functionalists

Today, both methodological and logical behaviourism are widely regarded as over-reactions to the subjectivist view of the mind. There is something slightly crazy about the view that mental states can never be known about introspectively, but only by observation of public behaviour.

Have you heard the joke about the two Behaviourists?

Nowadays, behaviourism in psychology has largely been superseded by **functionalism**. This upholds behaviourism's resistance to an essentially subjective conception of mental states, but at the same time allows that mental states can be *internal*, not necessarily displayed in public behaviour.

The trick is to think of mental states as internal items identified in terms of their typical causes and effects. Functionalists think of mental states as **causal** intermediaries, arising from perceptual stimuli, and only affecting behaviour via their interaction with other mental states.

So pain, for example, would be a state which typically arises from bodily damage, and typically causes a desire to avoid the source of that damage – with any resulting behaviour then depending on the interaction of this desire with other beliefs and desires.

*Functionalism thus allows that mental states can be real, even when they don't manifest themselves **directly** in observable action.*

You might have other desires – such as a desire to conceal your presence – which causes you to suppress any sign of pain.

I don't care how much it hurts – keep quiet or we're done for.

However, although functionalism makes mental states internal, it doesn't revert to identifying them subjectively in terms of what they **feel** like. Functionalism may think of mental states as internal and unobservable, but it still regards them as objective parts of the causal-scientific world.

According to functionalism, mental states are similar to scientific **unobservables** – like atoms, or genes, or quarks.

They are postulated as hidden causes, unobservable to the naked eye, but real nonetheless, and known via their causes and effects, rather than via any feelings they may involve.

Structure Versus Physiology

Even though functionalism postulates mental states as causal intermediaries between perception and behaviour, it does not commit itself on
what mental states are **made of**. Psychologists influenced by functionalism turned inwards towards the brain and away from behaviour.

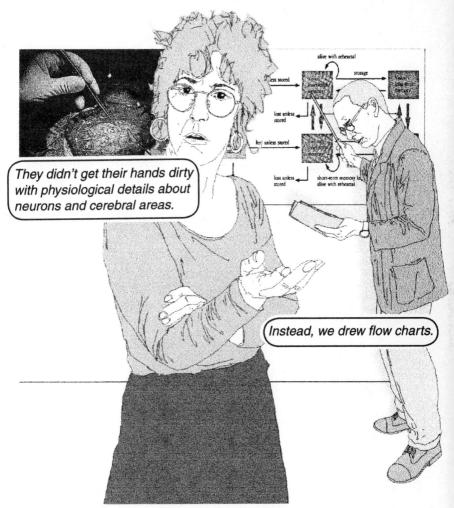

*They didn't get their hands dirty
with physiological details about
neurons and cerebral areas.*

Instead, we drew flow charts.

They hypothesized mental **structures** in abstraction from physiological
mechanisms. For functionalists, mental states were conceived abstractly,
in terms of the causal roles they play, rather than in terms of their material
make-up.

The Mind as the Brain's Software

An analogy is often drawn with the modern digital computer. We can distinguish the "hardware" of a computer from its "software". The "hardware" is the physical construction of the machine, the arrangement of silicon chips, or transistors, or radio valves, or indeed steel wheels and cogs, depending on what the computer is made of.

The "software" is the program that a machine is running – such as Microsoft Word, or Netscape, or Telnet.

Any given piece of software can run on machines with different hardware. Microsoft Word can run on both IBM PCs and Apple Macs, even though these machines have quite different physical constitutions. This is because the essence of the software is its **causal structure**.

The programmers have made sure that the relevant MS Word structure will be realized in both the PCs and the Macs.

What matters is that typing a word on the keyboard produces **some** internal state, which in turn produces appropriate responses on the VDU and the printer. It doesn't matter if the internal states in the PC and the Mac are different, as long as they both satisfy this structural requirement.

Variable Realization

Similarly, say functionalists, with the mind. When we talk about mental states, we are talking about software rather than hardware. That is, we are specifying a causal role, a **structure** of causes and effects, not the **materials** in which that role is realized. So we can think of the mind as the software and the brain as the hardware – or the "wetware", as it is sometimes called in this context.

This analogy has another implication.

Just as a given program, a piece of software, can be realized by different hardwares in different machines ...

... so can a given mental state, such as pain, be variably realized in the brains of different animals.

Humans and octopuses, for example, have quite different kinds of brains, made of quite different kinds of nerves. Yet, for functionalism, this doesn't stop them both being in pain.

For pain is a structural, software matter.

And the same structure can be variably realized in different materials.

Provided the human and the octopus are both in a state which typically arises from bodily damage, and typically causes a desire to avoid further damage, then they will both be in pain, even though different materials realize that state. It is just like two machines both running MS Word. Despite their different constitutions, they share the same structural properties.

A Physical Basis for Mind

Since functionalism doesn't commit itself on what mental states are made of, but only on structural matters, it is strictly consistent with dualism or even idealism. Maybe some special non-physical "mind-stuff" arises within the brains of conscious creatures, and fills the structural roles specified by functionalism. If this conscious mind-stuff has the right structure of causes and effects, then it will itself provide the basis for functionalist states of mind.

Pretty much all contemporary functionalists are materialists. They assume that the human mind is made solely of physical materials, not of any special mind-stuff.

After all, computers are made of nothing but matter, in the form of transistors and printed circuits, arranged into ingenious causal structures. Similarly, argue contemporary functionalists, we don't need anything apart from normal physical components, like nerves and synapses and neurotransmitters, to account for the causal structures typical of minds.

When we talk about minds, we are talking at the level of causal structure, and abstracting away from the details of mechanisms.

But, at the same time, contemporary functionalists see no reason to doubt that the mechanisms are physical – the components of your mind are made of matter, just as much as the components of your desktop computer.

A Modern Dualist Revival

Modern orthodoxy thus combines a **functionalist** view of mental roles with a **physicalist** account of how those roles are filled. Mental states are constituted by causal structures, and these structures are realized in humans and other creatures by physical mechanisms.

This modern orthodoxy highlights the "hard problem" of consciousness. It offers an entirely scientific, objective account of the mind, as a causal structure built of entirely physical materials.

One possible response to the hard problem is to insist that the mind must inhabit a separate non-physical realm after all. If modern orthodoxy represents humans as unfeeling, unthinking automata, then isn't this so much the worse for orthodoxy? It seems to be denying a crucial part of reality. A number of current philosophers, including David Chalmers, have urged that we reject this orthodoxy, and return to the Cartesian idea that this mental world is additional to the world of matter.

But modern dualists like Chalmers are less extreme than Descartes.

A Dualism of Properties

Modern dualists like Chalmers tend to avoid this "substance-dualism" and restrict themselves to a dualism of **properties**. Instead of thinking of conscious minds as made of a separate stuff, split off from the material body, they happily allow that humans are just one unified substance, and insist only that this single substance possesses two distinct kinds of properties.

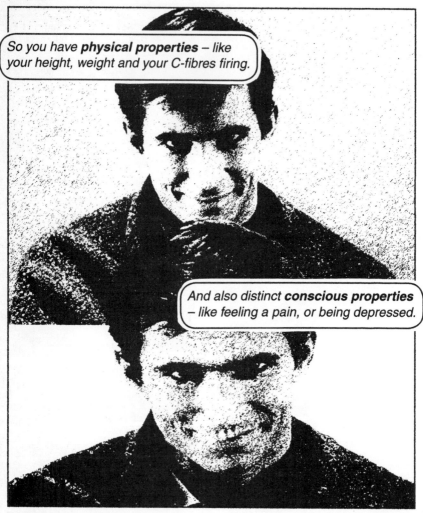

> *So you have **physical properties** – like your height, weight and your C-fibres firing.*

> *And also distinct **conscious properties** – like feeling a pain, or being depressed.*

In the philosophical jargon, modern dualists are "property-dualists" rather than "substance-dualists".

According to the modern dualist revival, behaviourism and functionalism were over-reactions to the excesses of idealism. They may have been understandable responses to the florid subjectivism of 19th-century philosophy. But viewing the mind as an entirely physical machine was surely going too far. Don't we all know, from our own case, that there is a non-physical, conscious essence to our minds?

The dualist revival can back up intuition with argument. In particular, recent dualists have used two well-known arguments to drive home the claim that mind must be distinct from matter. Both of these arguments have precursors in the original dualist writings of the 17th century.

One of the arguments – the argument from **possibility** – derives from Descartes.

The other – the argument from **knowledge** – was articulated by my successor, the great German philosopher **Gottfried Wilhelm von Leibniz** (1646–1716).

Descartes' Argument from Possibility

Descartes argued that it is perfectly possible for mind and body to exist separately. After all, there seems nothing contradictory in the idea of ghosts or immortal souls. Maybe there aren't any real ghosts, but surely it makes sense to suppose that you might continue to exist as a conscious being, even without your body. Certainly, millions of human beings have found much solace in this thought.

This possibility of posthumous survival implies that mind and body must be distinct, even if in reality they are always found together.

For, if they were the same thing, then what sense would there be to the idea of their coming apart?

A modern variant of this argument from possibility has been developed by the American philosopher Saul Kripke. This modern version deals with zombies rather than ghosts.

A Zombie Duplicate

Kripke imagines a being who is physically identical to himself – think of a perfect molecule-for-molecule duplicate made in a *Star Trek*-like holocopier – but who has no consciousness, no feelings of any kind.

Philosophers call this kind of human shell a "zombie". These philosophical "zombies" are rather different from the voodoo monsters familiar from B-movies. Voodoo zombies are the "living dead", soulless bodies animated by some evil spirit. This is why they lumber around so clumsily and often have difficulty avoiding the furniture.

Kripke's perfect physical duplicate is not supposed to be physically challenged in this way.

It behaves with the normal sophistication and dexterity of its human original.

After all, it has exactly the same arrangements of brain cells and motor nerves. It lacks only the **feelings**, the inner awareness.

Now, there are almost certainly no philosophical zombies in the actual universe. But Kripke's point does not require actual zombies. As with Descartes' argument, it is enough if it is **possible** for mind and brain to come apart. Whatever the practical difficulties of making a zombie, nothing obvious seems to rule out the possibility in principle. There doesn't seem anything logically contradictory in the idea of such a zombie. It is a being whose material body is like yours, but who has no feelings.

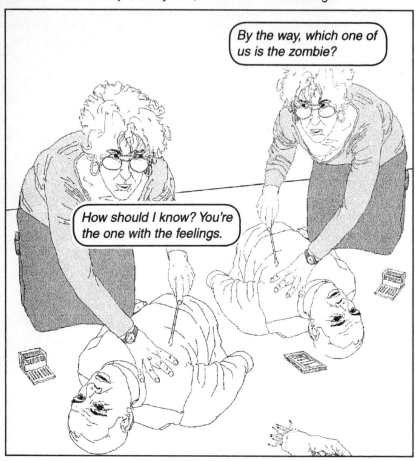

Yet, if zombies are possible, then conscious properties must be different from any physical or structural properties. For, by definition, your zombie shares all your physical and structural properties, yet lacks your conscious properties. So, if we so much as admit the zombie scenario as possible, its very description commits us to a difference between **conscious** properties and **physical** or **structural** properties.

Leibniz's Argument from Knowledge

The second argument for modern dualism trades in states of **knowledge** rather than states of **possibility**. An original version was articulated by Leibniz in his *Monadology* (first published 1840).

"Suppose that there be a machine, the structure of which produces thinking, feeling and perceiving; imagine this machine enlarged, but preserving the same proportion, so that you could enter it as if it were a mill. This being supposed, you might visit it inside; but what would you observe there? Nothing but parts which push and move each other, and never anything that could explain perception."

Leibniz's point is that even if you knew everything about the physical workings of the brain – as you might know the machinery of a mill – you still wouldn't know about consciousness. This seems to show that consciousness must be something different from physical mechanisms.

The Modern Argument from Knowledge

The modern version of Leibniz's argument comes from the Australian philosopher, Frank Jackson, and hinges on a science-fiction story about Mary, an expert psychologist who lives sometime in the future. Mary is an absolute authority on human vision and in particular on colour perception. She has complete scientific knowledge about what goes on in humans when they see colours.

She knows all about light waves and reflectance profiles, rods and cones, and the many areas concerned with vision in the occipital lobe, what they each do, how they combine, and so on.

She has never seen any colours herself. She has lived all her life inside a house painted black and white and shades of grey. All her knowledge of colour vision is "book learnin'" and none of her books contains any colour illustrations. She has a TV, but it is an old black-and-white set.

Then one day Mary walks out of her front door and sees a red rose. At this point, Jackson observes, Mary learns something new, something she didn't know before. She learns what it is **like** to see something red. If this is right, then it seems to follow once more that not all mental properties are physical or structural properties.

By hypothesis, I knew all about the physical and structural properties of colour experience before I walked out of my front door.

Yet, when she saw the rose, she learned about some further property of colour experience.

So this further property must be distinct from the physical and structural properties she already knew about. She has learned about the conscious aspect of red experience, about its phenomenal nature, about what it is like to see a red rose.

A Dualist Science of Consciousness

David Chalmers is one of those persuaded by these dualist arguments. He maintains that there is a separate phenomenal realm where conscious awareness can be found.

Chalmers does not regard this as a rejection of science, so much as a recommendation that science should expand its horizons.

Chalmers draws an analogy with the 19th-century recognition of electro-magnetism as a fundamental force. Originally, 19th-century scientists had hoped that electromagnetism could be explained in terms of more basic mechanical processes.

But **James Clerk Maxwell** (1831–79) and his contemporaries realized that this was impossible, and so added electromagnetism to the list of basic elements of reality. Chalmers urges exactly the same move with respect to consciousness.

Science needs to recognize a new basic feature of nature – the **phenomenal** – if it is to accommodate consciousness.

Chalmers envisages the construction of a theory which accounts for conscious phenomena. This theory would aim to specify the basic laws governing the emergence of conscious states, in just the way that Maxwell's theory specifies the laws governing electromagnetic fields.

Arguments Against Dualism

Before we come to detailed theories, though, there are philosophical problems facing any attempt to revive dualism. The most obvious is the problem of mind-body interaction. As we saw earlier, this problem is as old as dualism itself. It provoked Descartes' oft-ridiculed theory that mind and body interact in the pineal gland.

Modern dualism is a dualism of properties, not substances, and so avoids one of Descartes' problems – the problem of explaining how two quite different substances can communicate causally.

But the most awkward problem of mind-body interaction remains.

This is the problem of seeing how a mind can affect matter without violating the principles of physics themselves.

Causal Completeness

This is because the physical world appears to be **causally complete**. The causes of physical effects always seem to be other physical causes. If we trace back the causes of a goalkeeper rising to save a ball, say, we will find …

The Demise of Mental Forces

More generally, if we trace back the causes of physical effects, it seems that we will never have to leave the realm of the physical. And this seems to leave no room for non-physical properties, such as the conscious properties of experience, to make any difference to your behaviour. Since your behaviour is already fully accounted for by physical antecedents, any distinct conscious goings-on would seem to be casual danglers, themselves irrelevant to subsequent events.

The problem of squaring dualism with the causal completeness of physics is not entirely new. It was also widely recognized as a problem by 17th-century dualists. Surprisingly, Descartes himself seems not to have been worried by this aspect of mind-body interaction. But his immediate successors were not slow to point out that the deterministic physics of the 17th century ruled out any possibility of mind influencing matter.

Newtonian Physics

Curiously, this physics-based argument against dualism lost its force during the 18th and 19th centuries. This is because the austere physics of Descartes and Leibniz, in which all changes of material motion are due to contact between bodies, was replaced by the more liberal world view of **Sir Isaac Newton** (1642–1727).

Newtonian physics admits immaterial forces acting at a distance. The most famous of these is gravity. But Newton and his followers were prepared to admit many other such forces, like chemical forces and forces of adhesion.

And indeed special **vital** and **mental forces** which arise specifically in living creatures and intelligent animals, and help to direct the matter in their bodies.

It is only relatively recently that such special vital or mental forces have come to seem cranky. In the heyday of Newtonian science, such forces were part of the stock-in-trade of orthodox biologists and physiologists. They were regarded as no more mysterious than gravity or magnetism.

This idea of special "configurational" forces, which arise when matter is arranged in the complex patterns found in living bodies and intelligent brains, was preserved well into the 20th century. It is a central theme in the "emergentist" philosophy defended by **C.D. Broad** (1887–1971), author of *Mind and its Place in Nature* (1923) and Professor of Philosophy at Cambridge until 1953.

Back to Descartes

Physics has now moved back from Newtonian liberality to Cartesian austerity, and removed the mind from the class of causes with the power to move the body. True, we have not quite gone back to the original Cartesian view that all action is due to contact between bodies.

We still have forces which act at a distance.

And the chanciness of modern quantum mechanics means that we are no longer committed to physical determinism.

But physics again agrees with me on the crucial point.

The causes of material effects are always other material causes, not special mental or vital forces. Physics now recognizes three fundamental forces: the strong nuclear force, the electroweak force and gravity. According to contemporary physics, all non-random influences on the motion of matter are due to combinations of these forces. This leaves no room for an independent mind to make any material difference.

Materialist Physiology

A major influence discrediting special mental forces has been physiological research over the last 150 years. To a casual observer, it may seem obvious that we need some non-physical influence, with distinctive powers of consciousness and rational thought, to account for the elaborate speech and insightful decision-making of human beings.

It seems scarcely credible that a mere physical system could display the subtle behaviour found in human beings.

But this is just what modern physiological research suggests.

An awful lot is now known about what goes on inside the brain. During the first half of the 20th century, neurophysiologists mapped the body's neuronal network and analysed the electrical mechanisms responsible for neuronal activity. And since then, a great deal more has become known about the chemistry of nerve cells, and especially about the neurotransmitter molecules which such cells use to communicate with each other.

No Separate Mental Causes

Of course, this detailed physiological research still leaves a great deal to be understood, especially about how all the bits fit together to direct intelligent behaviour. But it does make it seem unlikely that there are special mental force fields.

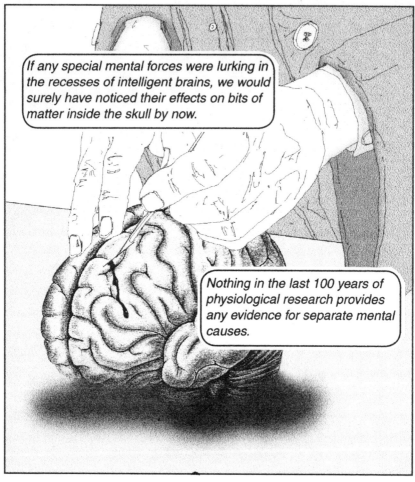

If any special mental forces were lurking in the recesses of intelligent brains, we would surely have noticed their effects on bits of matter inside the skull by now.

Nothing in the last 100 years of physiological research provides any evidence for separate mental causes.

There have been a few late 20th-century hold-outs prepared to deny the causal completeness of physics. Two of the most eminent physiologists of the century, the Nobel prizewinners **Sir John Eccles** (1903–97) and **Roger Sperry** (1913–94), both defended this line. They maintained that the conscious mind is separate from the brain and sometimes exerts an independent influence on its operations.

But few thinkers at the end of the 20th century still believe this. The idea of independent mental influences may once have been respectable, but by now the evidence against them seems overwhelming. Of course, modern physics may well be wrong about its precise current list of fundamental forces. Maybe there will turn out to be more than three fundamental forces – or a few less.

*But it seems very unlikely that one of the independent influences on material motion will turn out to be **mental.***

Imagine what it would be like if conscious minds sometimes exerted an independent influence on material motion.

Bits of matter in the brain – neurotransmitter molecules perhaps – would sometimes accelerate in ways that could not be accounted for by orthodox physics. The idea is not incoherent. But if it were true, modern physical science would be very surprised indeed.

What About Quantum Indeterminism?

Doesn't the indeterminism of modern quantum mechanics create a loophole which allows the mind to make a material difference?

According to quantum mechanics, many physical events, including events in the brain, are not **determined** by prior physical causes. At most, the prior physical causes fix the **probabilities** for various possible results. **Albert Einstein** (1879–1955) hated this idea.

Still, this quantum mechanical indeterminism doesn't really help dualism. As long as prior physical causes so much as fix the **probabilities** of physical results, independent mental influences will still be ruled out.

Imagine, for the sake of argument, that independent conscious events — conscious decisions, perhaps — did take advantage of the indeterministic space created by quantum mechanics to influence the movements of neurotransmitters in the brain. Then presumably such neurotransmitter movements would occur more often when preceded by those conscious decisions than when not.

Otherwise, why suppose that the conscious decisions were exerting any influence on the neurotransmitters in the first place?

But this now means that the probabilities wouldn't be fixed by physical causes after all.

God's dice game would be rigged. Conscious decisions would be loading the dice. Less metaphorically, independent conscious causes would be affecting the probabilities of physical results. This would be a violation of the quantum version of the causal completeness of physics, the principle that the probabilities of physical results are fixed by prior physical causes alone. As before, this possibility is not incoherent. But, once more, modern physical science would be very surprised indeed if it turned out to be true.

Causal Impotence

Most contemporary dualists adopt a different line in the face of the causal completeness of physics. They simply accept that the mental does not, after all, exert any causal influence on the material world. It might seem like the merest common sense to suppose that our conscious feelings and sufferings, our hopes and decisions, affect the movements of our bodies, and hence the rest of the physical world.

But contemporary dualists are prepared to accept that this is an illusion.

Since there is no room for anything non-physical to affect physical results, we accept that the conscious mind must be "causally impotent".

We are indeed like the child with a toy steering-wheel. We think we are running the show, but we are not.

Pre-established Harmony

An early version of this position was developed in the 17th century by Leibniz. Recall that Leibniz urged the causal completeness of the physical world against Descartes. Leibniz concluded that mind and matter cannot really influence each other, and that the appearance of interaction must be due to **pre-established harmony**. By this Leibniz meant that God must have arranged things to make sure that mind and matter always keep in step. In reality they do not interact, like two trains running on separate tracks.

But God fixed their starting times and speeds to ensure that they would always run smoothly alongside each other.

Events on the mental and physical trains remain in synchrony with each other.

God's plan ensures that conscious decisions are always followed by appropriate physical movements, and sitting on a drawing pin is always followed by a conscious pain.

Modern Epiphenomenalism

Modern dualists prefer a rather simpler way of keeping mind and matter in step. This is **epiphenomenalism**, which does not require advance planning by an omniscient being.

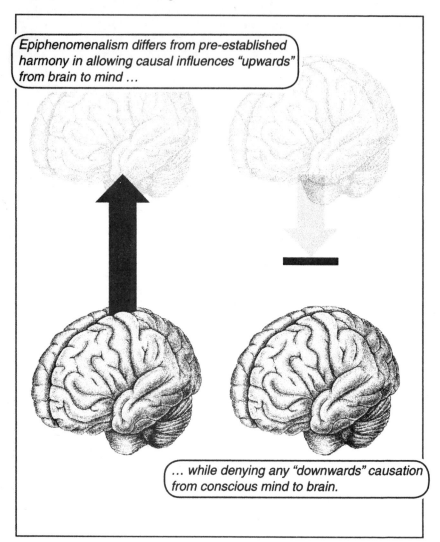

Epiphenomenalism differs from pre-established harmony in allowing causal influences "upwards" from brain to mind ...

... while denying any "downwards" causation from conscious mind to brain.

This respects the causal completeness of physics: nothing non-physical causally influences the physical brain. But it avoids Leibniz's theological complications by allowing the brain itself to cause conscious effects.

According to epiphenomenalism, the conscious mind is an "epiphenomenon" of the brain, a "dangler" caused by the brain, but with no power to influence the brain in return. The brain is influenced by prior physical causes alone. Everything in the brain would work the same, even if it did not give rise to conscious mental experience. As it happens, it does give rise to conscious experience, but this makes no difference to its physical workings.

But at the same time, it emits puffs of immaterial "mental smoke" which are real enough at the conscious level, but make no difference to the subsequent motion of the train.

The Oddity of Epiphenomenalism

Epiphenomenalism is not a particularly attractive position. It implies, for instance, that the conscious thirst you feel on a hot day plays no part in causing you to go to the fridge for a beer. Since your going to the fridge is a physical event, and as such entirely due to physical causes in your brain, the distinct conscious thirst cannot influence your action.

Epiphenomenalism has even more surprising consequences. If conscious mental states don't have any influence on our behaviour, then it follows that our behaviour would continue just the same, even if we were zombies – even if the activities in our brain were unaccompanied by any conscious feelings.

Yet, by hypothesis, we wouldn't have any conscious experiences ourselves. Our zombie mouths would simply be driven by the same physical processes that drive normal human mouths. David Chalmers makes the point graphically. He points out that his zombie counterpart would carry on just like the actual David Chalmers.

"He talks about conscious experience all the time - in fact he seems obsessed by it. He spends ridiculous amounts of time hunched over a computer, writing chapter after chapter on the mysteries of consciousness. He often comments on the pleasure he gets from certain sensory qualia, professing a particular love for deep greens and purples. He frequently gets into arguments with zombie materialists, arguing that their position cannot do justice to the realities of conscious experience. And yet he has no conscious experience at all!" (Chalmers, *The Conscious Mind*.)

The Materialist Alternative

It is hard to accept the epiphenomenalist doctrine that our conscious experience plays no part in causing our behaviour. This doctrine seems especially absurd when applied to the verbal behaviour which we normally interpret as describing our conscious experiences.

Still, is there any alternative?

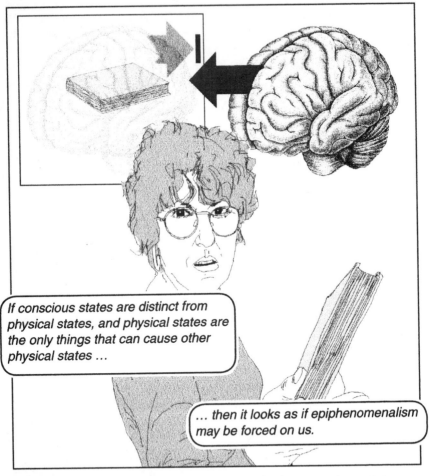

If conscious states are distinct from physical states, and physical states are the only things that can cause other physical states …

… then it looks as if epiphenomenalism may be forced on us.

The most popular alternative is to query whether conscious states are really distinct from physical states to start with. This is the **materialist** option. Its obvious virtue is that it promises to restore causal potency to conscious experience.

If conscious states *are* just physical brain states, then they will have all the physical effects that those brain states have. Nor need we be puzzled by zombies who prattle away about their experiences.

So materialism promises to avoid the drawbacks of epiphenomenalism. Is materialism a real option, though? What about the earlier arguments, due to Saul Kripke and Frank Jackson, which aimed to establish that conscious states *must* be different from brain states? We will need to re-examine these arguments, if materialism is to prove an alternative to epiphenomenalism.

Materialism is not Elimination

But first it will be helpful to be clearer on what materialism says. It is important to recognize that normal materialists do not want to **eliminate** conscious experience. They do not deny that it is **like something** to be in pain, that unpleasant **feelings** occur when we sit on a pin.

Their claim is only that these feelings are nothing different from the relevant brain states.

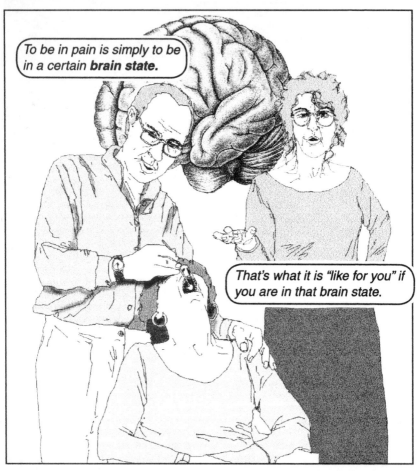

Materialists can appeal to a different analogy from 19th-century physics to set against David Chalmers' dualist appeal to electromagnetic theory. Where Chalmers appeals to electromagnetism, they can appeal to temperature.

The Example from Temperature

In the case of temperature, physicists went the other way. Instead of adding temperature to the fundamental components of reality, they explained it in terms of a more basic mechanical quantity, namely **mean kinetic energy**.

Note that this did not eliminate temperature from our world view, in the way that "animal spirits", say, have been eliminated, or "vital forces". We still think temperature exists all right.

> We just don't think of temperature as something **extra** to **mean kinetic energy**, in the way that electromagnetic fields are **extra** to the motions of charged particles.

Similarly with consciousness, urge the materialists. Conscious states exist all right, but not as something extra to brain activity. Just as we have discovered that temperature is nothing but mean kinetic energy, so, argue the reductionists, we should accept that conscious states, like pain, are nothing but certain brain states.

Functionalist Materialism

Exactly what kind of brain states do materialists want to equate conscious experience with? **Functionalist** materialists, like the American philosopher-psychologist **Jerry Fodor** (b. 1935) and many others, want to equate conscious experience with structural properties, rather than with strictly physical or physiological properties.

Recall that functionalists equate the mind with software, rather than hardware or "wetware".

Just as computers of different constructions can run the same software program, creatures with different physiologies can share the same kind of conscious experience.

That's why humans and octopuses can both feel pain, even though they are physically quite different.

This is because they can both share the **structural** property of being in **some** physical state (though a different physical state in each case) which arises from bodily damage and causes a desire to avoid further damage.

Similarly, as-yet-undiscovered extra-terrestrials, with an alien silicon-based metabolism, could also satisfy the functionalist requirements for being in pain, as long as they shared the appropriate structural property.

So functionalism equates conscious properties with structural properties. Many theorists, however, find this equation implausible.

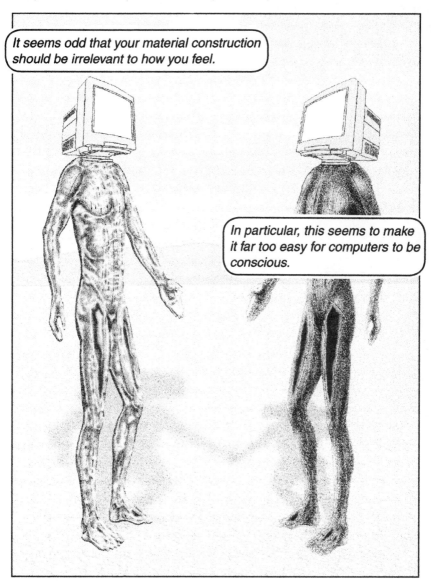

Making a Computer Conscious?

In principle, we can structure – that is, program – a large enough digital computer to realize any causal structure whatever. So we could give it internal states which played just the same causal role in it as pains do in us. And similarly for the causal roles played by emotions, itches, and thoughts about life after death.

It is hard to believe that there could be something that it is "like" to be a computer, even one structured in the right way.

And remember that it's not supposed to matter what the computer is made of. You may be happy with the idea of a streamlined, super-duper, talking computer being conscious, like HAL in Stanley Kubrick's classic sci-fi film *2001*.

But you need to ask yourself, what would you say if the same causal structures were realized in an older-fashioned computer?

Indeed, we could presumably realize the same structures in a sufficiently ingenious Heath-Robinson arrangement of old beer cans and bicycle wheels. Could it really "feel like" something to be a scrap-metal machine?

The Turing Test

The British mathematician and inventor of the modern computer, **Alan Turing** (1912–54), believed that intelligent computers would be built fairly soon. In support of this conjecture, he devised the "Turing Test" as a criterion for computer consciousness.

Imagine you are communicating with some being via some remote device, like a telex or e-mail. You can't tell directly if you are talking to a machine or a person, because you can't see it. But you can ask it questions, discuss its responses, and so on.

Your task is to decide whether you are communicating with a human or not.

If a machine can trick you into thinking it is a person, then it passes the "Turing Test".

And anything that can pass this test, argued Alan Turing, ought to be credited with the same kind of consciousness as we have.

But to many people this seems absurd. How can a mere computer, even a sophisticated one, feel anything? A computer that passes the Turing Test may be **simulating** a conscious mind.

The "Chinese Room Argument", developed by the American philosopher John Searle, drives home this worry about mere facts of computer organization sufficing for conscious mentality. This is the argument we shall next examine.

The Chinese Room

Searle imagines a man sitting inside a closed room. Every so often a piece of paper covered with squiggly marks is passed through a hole in the wall. The man in the room then consults a huge manual, which tells him that if certain squiggly marks come in, then a piece of paper with certain other squiggly marks on it should be passed out again.

Unknown to the man in the room, the squiggles in question are all Chinese writing.

And the squiggles he passes out, as instructed by the manual, are always good Chinese answers to the Chinese questions on the incoming slips.

Now, despite this, the man in the room clearly does not understand Chinese. From his point of view, the squiggles are all meaningless, and he is simply following the manual's instructions blindly.

But note that the man in the room is doing just what a well-programmed digital computer does. He is responding to inputs with appropriate outputs in a causally systematic way.

Still, this would be a mistaken assumption. So the Turing Test does not seem to guarantee a conscious mind after all. It seems to mistake the *appearance* of consciousness for the real thing.

Language and Consciousness

Strictly speaking, the Chinese Room Argument is directed against a functionalist account of linguistic understanding, rather than against the functionalist account of consciousness. Still, understanding a language is an **intentional** (that is, representational) notion, and intentionality and consciousness are closely related, as we shall see later.

Searle himself certainly takes it that linguistic understanding requires consciousness experience.

So the Chinese Room Argument can operate as a challenge to the functionalist account of consciousness, as well as to its account of linguistic understanding.

Not all functionalists capitulate to the Chinese Room Argument. They point out that the crucial issue is not whether the man inside understands the inscriptions – clearly he doesn't – but whether the whole system does. After all, the Chinese Room is presumably supposed to establish the non-consciousness of whole computers, not of every component.

Even those who think that computers are conscious don't think that every transistor inside them is a centre of consciousness.

Moreover, observe the functionalists, any Chinese Room that really could answer all those Chinese questions would presumably need various sensors, mechanical eyes and ears, to update its information about its current environment. Given this, however, it no longer seems so clear that the system doesn't know what it is talking about, that it doesn't know, for example, what the Chinese symbol for "rain" is.

Functionalist Epiphobia

Let us leave the Chinese Room at this stage, though. For there is a more basic reason for not wanting to follow functionalists in equating conscious states with structural ones.

Remember that the unique selling point of materialism was that it promised to restore causal power to conscious states. By identifying conscious properties with brain properties, we hoped to cure the impotence associated with epiphenomenalism.

But will this be achieved if we identify conscious properties with *structural properties*, rather than the more down-to-earth physiological states which realize those structures in different organisms?

*After all, it is presumably the passage of specific human neurotransmitters across my synapses which **causes** my arm muscles to contract.*

Not some more abstract structural property which I may share with octopuses.

This worry has caused many recent functionalists to come down with "epiphobia". This is the (all too rational) fear that functionalism may unwittingly be condemning mental states to the same causal impotence as epiphenomenalism.

Functionalists identify human pain with some structural property which we share with octopuses. This structural property must be distinct from any specific physiological property, since humans and octopuses have different physiologies.

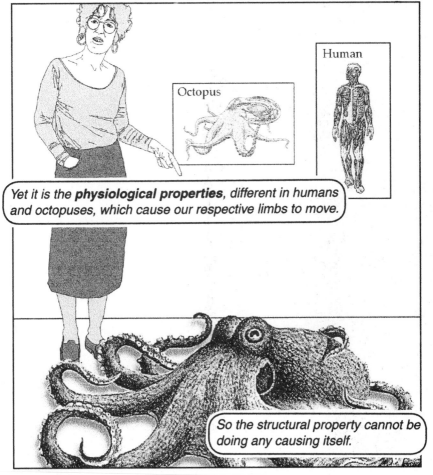

Octopus

Human

*Yet it is the **physiological properties**, different in humans and octopuses, which cause our respective limbs to move.*

So the structural property cannot be doing any causing itself.

Functionalists thus seem to end up on the same side as epiphenomenalism, viewing the pain itself as a puff of smoke, emitted by the train of real causation, but inefficacious in itself.

Mental States are "Wetware"

Epiphobia has turned many recent materialist philosophers of mind away from functionalism, and towards an outright identification of pains and other mental states with physiological states. Mental states are hardware after all, or at least "wetware", not software.

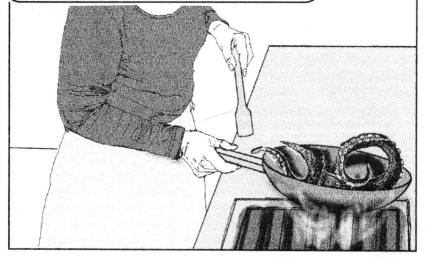

This move also has the virtue of blocking the Chinese Room and other anti-software arguments.

If materialists no longer identify feelings with structural software properties, but with specific kinds of "wetware", they can ignore arguments designed to show that software in itself cannot guarantee consciousness.

Human Chauvinism

There is a cost to this reaction against functionalism, however. Materialists now seem committed to a kind of **chauvinism**, for they hold that beings with different physiologies cannot share our feelings. One of the original attractions of functionalism was that it allowed interspecific feelings.

Octopuses could have just the same pains as humans.

But this is ruled out, once we equate human pains with wetware rather than software.

Still, perhaps materialists can live with this. They don't have to deny that octopuses have unpleasant feelings of any kind. It is only that they now distinguish them from human pains. Put like this, it doesn't seem so crazy. It seems all right to distinguish human pains from octopus pains, if this is the price of restoring their causal powers.

Facing up to the Dualist Arguments

Materialists, of any stripe, still need to face up to the dualist arguments developed by Saul Kripke and Frank Jackson. In this context, it doesn't matter whether materialists identify mental properties with structural properties or with physiological ones. They are under pressure either way.

So it doesn't matter whether materialists opt for structural or physiological properties. Kripke and Jackson threaten both kinds of materialism.

Still, materialists have an answer. They can say that Kripke and Jackson only establish a difference at the level of **concepts**, not a difference at the level of the **properties** themselves. Materialists will allow that we have two different ways of thinking *about* mental properties: we can think of them *as* conscious, and we can think of them *as* material. But materialists will deny that there are actually two properties here, as opposed to one property thought about in two ways.

Think of cases where one person has two names.

You can think of me as Judy Garland or as Frances Gumm.

We have two ways of thinking, but this doesn't mean there are two people we think about.

Again, take the example of temperature and mean kinetic energy. Children are first taught to think of degree of heat in terms of temperature. After they learn some science, they might think of it as mean kinetic energy. These are two ways of thinking, but there is just one quantity in reality.

This is how materialists will deal with the Mary example. They will admit that there is a genuine "before-after" difference when Mary first steps out of her front door. But they will say that this is just a matter of Mary acquiring a new *concept* of "seeing red", a new way of *thinking* about the experience.

Now that Mary has actually seen red, she can imagine it. Before, she couldn't do this.

But this doesn't mean that she couldn't think about the experience at all before she had it. What she now thinks about imaginatively is still the same experience she could previously think about scientifically.

The availability of two kinds of concepts for thinking about experience confuses us into thinking that zombies are possible, even when they aren't.

The existence of two kinds of concepts makes us think that we can describe a being who both *has* and *lacks* experiences.

We use our concepts of structural and physiological properties to set up the basic idea of a zombie who is functionally and physically identical to a normal human. Then we use our **imaginative concepts** of experience to deny the zombie consciousness. But in fact we are postulating a contradiction. Since conscious properties are material properties, zombies are impossible.

Zombies are Impossible

According to materialists, Kripke is like someone who doesn't realize that Judy Garland and Frances Gumm are the same person, and so insists that one woman can be somewhere the other isn't. Or he is like an insufficiently educated student who thinks it possible for two samples of gas to be at the same temperature, yet to have different mean kinetic energies. These things seem possible, but are not.

Similarly, urge materialists, with zombies. They seem possible, but are not.

Not even God could make a zombie.

From the dualist's point of view, God's work was not done when He had finished constructing our physical bodies. He still needed to put the feelings in. So He could, if He had wished, have left us as zombies by downing tools at that stage, and leaving the feelings out.

There wasn't any possibility of God quitting work at the zombie stage. Once He had fixed the bodily parts, He would therewith have fixed the feelings. A body without feelings is beyond even an omnipotent God.

Mysteries of Consciousness

This materialist line does not persuade everybody. Identifying mind and brain seems far less plausible than identifying Judy Garland and Frances Gumm, or even temperature and mean kinetic energy.

Given evidence that Judy went everywhere that Frances went, and that mean kinetic energy plays just the same causal role as temperature, then any sensible person will accept that these things are identical. But with mind and brain it seems different.

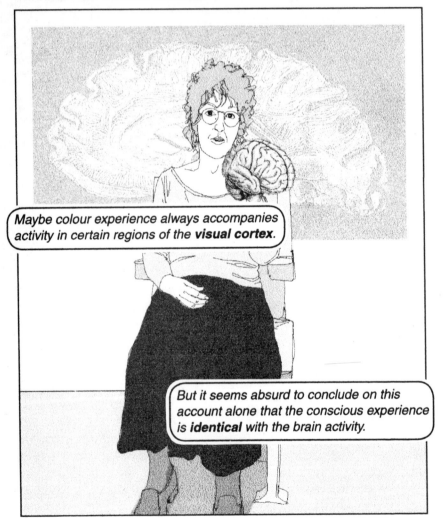

Maybe colour experience always accompanies activity in certain regions of the **visual cortex**.

But it seems absurd to conclude on this account alone that the conscious experience is **identical** with the brain activity.

The British philosopher Colin McGinn is one of those who finds the identity impossible to stomach. "How can technicolour phenomenology arise from soggy grey matter?" he asks. For McGinn, it beggars belief that our vibrant awareness of bright colours could simply be the same thing as neurons firing off deep in our gelatinous brains.

A number of other philosophers, including Thomas Nagel (remember the bats), share McGinn's disbelief. While Nagel appreciates the reasons for wanting to identify mind and brain, he argues that we lack any conception of how they *could* be identical.

At the same time, these anti-materialist philosophers do not want to return to dualism.

They accept that a distinct realm of non-material conscious states would lack any causal power over matter, and thus that Dualism cannot avoid the absurdities of epiphenomenalism.

The Mysterian Position

Given this dilemma, they conclude that the problem of consciousness lies beyond human comprehension. It is too hard for us to solve. We can't live with an identity between conscious and physical ones, but we can't live without one either (unless we accept mental impotence). It is a mystery. These "mysterian" philosophers suggest that we lack the right concepts to understand the issue. Our notions of mental and physical are too crude to allow any real insight into the mind-body relation.

Maybe the reason why we can't understand consciousness is the same as the reason why monkeys can't do differential calculus. The requisite concepts are just beyond us.

A Mysterian Speculation

McGinn himself is not afraid to speculate about what we might be missing. He suggests that reality may have been non-spatial in the time before the Big Bang. With the Big Bang, space came into being.

Perhaps consciousness is a resurrection of the non-spatial reality from the earlier epoch.

Once complex enough brains evolved, this somehow enabled the non-spatial dimension to re-emerge into the modern world as consciousness, a kind of immaterial fossil from the time before the Big Bang.

Special Concepts of Consciousness

Are such flights of fancy as McGinn's necessary? Materialists will object that the mysterians have given up too quickly. They have given us no good reason not to keep our feet on the ground of mind-brain identity. In the end, their case rests on nothing more than their blank incredulity at the idea that "soggy grey matter" might constitute "technicolour phenomenology".

Of course, materialists can agree, this mind-brain equation is highly counter-intuitive.

It is much harder to believe than other identities.

People continue to resist it, even after any amount of evidence showing that mind and brain always go hand in hand.

Still, perhaps, materialists can offer an explanation of why mind-brain activity should seem so counter-intuitive, even if it is true. They can appeal to the special kind of imaginative concepts that we use when we think about mental items *as* conscious.

These are concepts like the one Mary acquires when she leaves her shadowy house and sees red for the first time. She acquires the ability, which she lacked before, to think about the experience by recreating it in her imagination. It is a particularly vivid way of thinking about conscious experiences. This is why other ways of thinking about conscious states seem anaemic by comparison. According to materialism, colour experience is identical to activity in the visual cortex. But we can think of it either **as** cortical activity ("soggy grey matter") or by **re-enacting** the experience ("technicolour phenomenology").

And so, naturally enough, when we think of it in the former way, we feel that we are somehow leaving out the experience itself, since we aren't re-enacting it.

This doesn't mean that the cortical thought ("soggy grey matter") isn't **about** the same thing as the imaginative thought.

There is every reason to suppose that these two concepts refer to the same thing.

We shouldn't allow ourselves to be distracted from this sensible conclusion by the peculiar fact that we have a special way of thinking about conscious experiences – namely, by re-enacting them.

Everybody Wants a Theory

So far the discussion of the mind-brain relation has proceeded at a pretty abstract level. We have asked whether the conscious mind is identical to the brain – materialism – or whether it constitutes an extra realm of reality – dualism – or whether the whole thing is too hard to understand anyway – mysterianism.

But we haven't stopped to inquire about which **bits** of the brain might be associated with consciousness. Exactly which parts of the brain yield conscious experience? It is obvious enough that not all parts do. There are plenty of processes occurring in the brain which have no conscious counterpart, from the production of hormones to the regulation of breathing.

We need a **theory of consciousness**.

> *Such a theory would tell us what is required for consciousness.*

> *It would distinguish those brain activities which yield consciousness from those which do not.*

> *With luck, such a theory ought to be able to tell us which animals are conscious.*

Once the theory has identified the kinds of brain processes which yield consciousness, then we should be able to check whether similar processes occur in cats, or fish, or snails. In fact, however, these comparisons are not always straightforward, as we shall see.

Somewhat curiously, the search for a theory of consciousness in this sense is independent of whether you are a materialist, a dualist or even a mysterian. Whichever of these metaphysical positions you adopt, you can still be interested in identifying those physical processes that suffice to yield consciousness.

Of course, materialists will want to **identify** phenomenal consciousness with these physical processes, whereas dualists will think of consciousness as something **extra** which accompanies the physical processes, and mysterians will say the issue is **too hard** to understand.

But this divergence makes little difference to the shape of the theories which are developed. Whatever the metaphysics, the aim is an identification of those brain processes that yield consciousness.

Indeed, proponents of "theories of consciousness" are not always clear about whether they are thinking in materialist, dualist, or other terms.

It is not uncommon to find such theorists introducing their theories with explicit disavowals of dualism.

Yet quickly slipping into talk about the physical processes which "generate" consciousness, or "cause" it, or "give rise to" it.

Talk which only really makes sense from a dualist point of view.

Still, we needn't fuss about this, given that the search for a theory of consciousness can proceed independently of the choice between materialism, dualism and mysterianism. From now on I shall ignore the metaphysical dispute, and concentrate on the shared ambition to identify the physical processes which yield consciousness.

Neural Oscillations

Many scientists from different fields are currently pursuing the holy grail of a theory of consciousness. One of them is the co-discoverer of DNA, the Nobel prizewinning biochemist Francis Crick. Working in collaboration with psychologist Christof Koch, Crick has developed the theory that the key to consciousness lies in striking patterns of neural oscillations found in the visual cortex in the range 35–75 Hertz.

According to Crick and Koch, these oscillations are the brain's solution to "the binding problem".

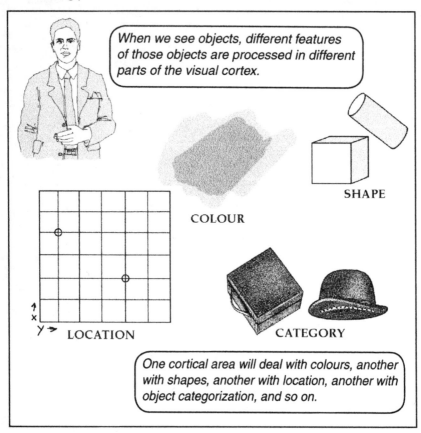

So, if you see a cubic green box to the left, and a cylindrical red hat to the right, you will register red and green in the **colour** area, cubical and cylindrical in the **shape** area, left and right in the **location** area, box and hat in the **categorization** area.

This creates an apparent problem. How do we "bind" the cubic left-hand green box back together again? To get beyond an unstructured awareness of red and green, left and right, and so on, it seems that we must somehow put "cubic" together again with "green", "box", and "left", rather than with "red", "hat" and "right".

This is where the oscillations help. The different aspects of one object are all associated with brain waves which are at the same frequency in the 35–75 Hertz range, and which are in phase (the peaks and troughs occur at the same time). The different aspects of other objects will similarly be associated with binding brain waves, but with different frequencies and phases. These signature waves thus enable the brain to keep track of which visual features should be bound together to constitute our visual awareness of objects.

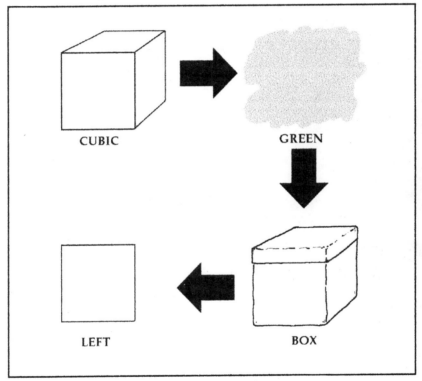

More generally, Crick and Koch argue that these binding oscillations are the "neural correlate" of visual consciousness. On their theory, it is the unifying role played by these brain waves that accounts for our conscious visual awareness.

Neural Darwinism

The American physiologist Gerald Edelman is another eminent Nobel prizewinner who has turned to consciousness towards the end of his career, hoping to cap his earlier successes with one last great achievement.

Edelman views the brain from the perspective of "neural Darwinism".

The brain starts off with an overabundance of neural connections. Those which are not encouraged by neural stimulation wither and die.

In human beings, 70% of the neurons that we start off with have disappeared by the age of eight months.

The result of this neural evolution, according to Edelman, is a system of interconnected neural "maps", each responsible for different aspects of visual and other perception. When the brain receives some new stimulus, many different maps will become activated and start sending signals to each other.

Re-entrant Loops

Such patterns of interconnected activity Edelman calls "re-entrant loops". These "re-entrant" neural circuits continue to evolve as experience accumulates, and the connections between neurons are subject to further neural natural selection.

Edelman regards this evolving structure of re-entrant loops as the basis of conscious awareness. The connections between the maps constitute a form of memory, and this contributes to the perceptual categorization of incoming information. Re-entrant loops also play a part, argues Edelman, in thinking and reasoning, and in the control of behaviour.

Evolution and Consciousness

Speaking of Darwin, it might seem as if his general theory of the evolution of species by natural selection could help to throw some useful light on consciousness.

Thinking about the evolutionary purpose of some trait often helps us better to understand it. Once we know that the evolutionary purpose of the heart is to pump the blood, say, or that the evolutionary purpose of saliva is to help digest food, then we are much better placed to understand these traits.

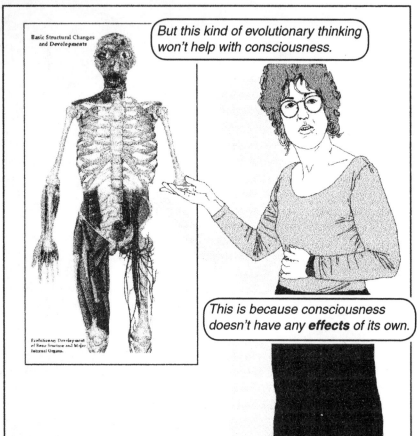

Basic Structural Changes and Developments

Evolutionary Development of Bone Structure and Major Internal Organs.

But this kind of evolutionary thinking won't help with consciousness.

*This is because consciousness doesn't have any **effects** of its own.*

Both materialists and (epiphenomenalist) dualists agree that conscious properties do not produce any bodily effects, apart from those produced in any case by the brain.

Yet evolutionary understanding trades in effects. To identify the evolutionary purpose of a trait is to identify some effect which benefits survival.

We have hearts nowadays because blood-pumping hearts aided our ancestors.

We salivate nowadays because salivation helped our ancestors to digest food.

This means that evolution is not going to explain why certain brain processes yield consciousness, while others don't.

Evolution could only do this if consciousness had some extra survival-enhancing effects, beyond those caused anyway by brain processes. But consciosness doesn't have any such effects. Our ancestors didn't survive because their brain processes generated consciousness. They would have survived just as well even if they had been zombies. Their brains would have produced the same physical effects anyway.

The Purpose of Consciousness

Of course, materialist philosophers of mind, who **identify** consciousness with certain brain processes, will hold that consciousness does in a sense have effects – namely, the effects produced by those brain processes. So in this sense materialists at least will be able to ascribe biological purposes to consciousness.

But note that, even for such materialists, this won't help decide **which** brain processes yield consciousness in the first place.

In order for materialists to know about the evolutionary purposes of **consciousness**, as opposed to other brain activities, they first need to know which brain activities constitute consciousness and which don't. They need a theory of consciousness *before* evolution can tell them anything about the purpose of consciousness. The appeal to evolution thus only takes them round in a circle.

Quantum Collapses

There is one rather speculative approach which does regard consciousness as having its own effects. This is the view that ties consciousness to quantum phenomena, and in particular to the "collapse" of quantum wave functions.

Quantum mechanics is a very odd theory. The indeterminism ("God playing dice") is only a small part of the oddity.

Indeed, much of quantum mechanics is not indeterministic at all.

*For the most part, quantum mechanics describes physical systems in terms of **wave functions** which evolve deterministically, in accord with my equation.*

$$\frac{\partial^2 \psi}{\partial x^2} + \frac{8\pi^2 m}{h^2} \left(E - V\right) \psi = 0$$

Erwin Schrödinger (1887-1961)

In this respect, quantum mechanics is like classical mechanics in earlier physics, whose laws of motion tell us how the positions and velocities of any system of particles will evolve deterministically through time.

How Quantum Physics Differs

The difference is that quantum wave functions don't **specify** positions and velocities as such, but **probabilities** of particles turning out to have certain positions and velocities when a "measurement" is made.

The real oddity of quantum mechanics is not its indeterminism, but that it offers no real understanding of such "measurements".

Measurements somehow cause quantum waves – which standardly admit various alternative positions and velocities – to "collapse" indeterministically into definite values.

This kind of change, however, is not predicted by Schrödinger's equation. It is a matter of extreme controversy how it should best be understood.

Schrödinger's Cat

The famous thought-experiment involving "Schrödinger's cat" makes the issue graphic. The poor cat is placed in a sealed box, together with a capsule of poison gas. The capsule is rigged up so that it will emit the poison gas if an electron fired from an electron gun hits the top half of a sensitive detector screen, but not if it hits the bottom half.

The electron gun's aim is indeterministic.

E

POISON GAS

The wave function of this overall physical system gives the electron an equal chance of hitting the top and the bottom halves of the screen. So the cat's fate is not sealed until this wave function "collapses", and it is decided which half of the screen the electron hits.

But when does this happen? When does the wave function collapse? When do things become definite? When the electron hits the screen? When the cat first breathes poison or air? Or only when the cat dies or survives? Schrödinger's equation itself doesn't tell us the answer. It is just as happy to view the cat as an indefinite "superposition" of alive and dead, as it is to view the electron as a "superposition" of an upwards trajectory and a downwards one.

*At some point, it seems, things must become definite. But the physics itself does not tell us **when**.*

Quantum Consciousness

One bold view is that quantum waves collapse only when they interact with consciousness. Nothing need be definite until it is perceived by a **conscious observer**. If this is right, then Schrödinger's cat is neither definitely alive nor dead until a conscious observer opens the box and looks inside. Unless, of course, cats are conscious themselves. In which case, things will become definite as soon as they register on the cat's consciousness.

The American physicist Henry Stapp is one of those who favours such an interpretation of quantum mechanics. Stapp argues that quantum waves collapse when intelligent brains select one among the alternative quantum possibilities as a basis for future action.

For Stapp, this interpretation of quantum mechanics is simultaneously a theory of consciousness. It is specifically the parts of the brain that are implicated in quantum collapses that constitute consciousness.

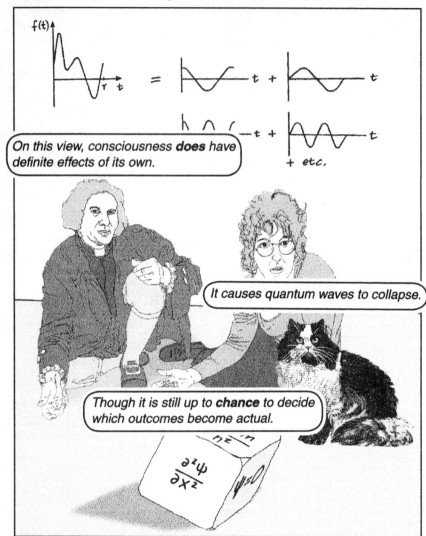

A conscious observation ensures that the cat has some definite fate, but God's dice still decide which fate that is – whether the cat turns up alive or dead. Stapp argues that this causal efficacy allows consciousness to serve a biological purpose. Its role is to eliminate alternative realities and thereby allow us better to plan our actions.

Another Link to Quantum Mechanics

Another thinker who links consciousness to quantum mechanics is Roger Penrose, Rouse Ball Professor of Mathematics at Oxford University. Penrose holds that consciousness is tied to activity in cytoskeletal microtubules, the cylindrical protein structures that provide the scaffolding for living cells, including brain neurons.

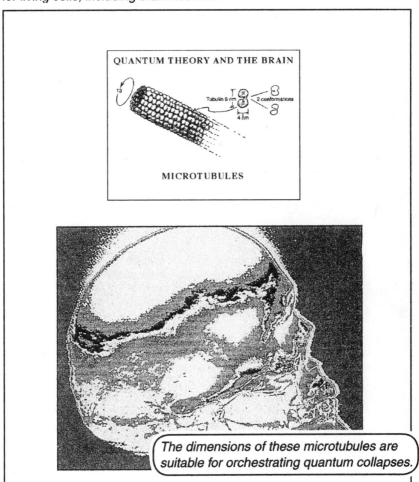

The dimensions of these microtubules are suitable for orchestrating quantum collapses.

Penrose has a rather different approach to quantum collapses from Stapp. He suggests that gravitational effects may be responsible. The role of microtubules is to channel quantum waves until they reach the gravitational threshold for collapses.

Quantum Collapses and Gödel's Theorem

So, for Penrose, consciousness is not an independent cause which triggers quantum collapses. Rather, it is simply the way in which such quantum collapses **manifest** themselves in our minds.

Kurt Gödel's (1906–78) famous theorem about the incompleteness of arithmetic also plays a role in Penrose's theory. Gödel's theorem shows that no axiom system is powerful enough to generate all the truths of arithmetic. According to Penrose, this shows that the human mind must somehow have "non-algorithmic" powers that go beyond axioms and rules.

Not all logicians agree about this inference, but this doesn't stop Penrose from suggesting that the non-algorithmicity of consciousness derives from its connection with quantum mechanics.

Even if we put Gödel's theorem to one side, there are other doubts about the supposed link between consciousness and quantum mechanics. Critics accuse thinkers like Stapp and Penrose of simply piling one mystery on top of another.

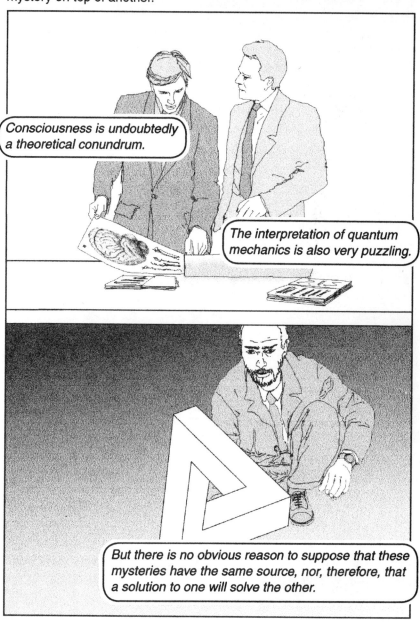

Consciousness is undoubtedly a theoretical conundrum.

The interpretation of quantum mechanics is also very puzzling.

But there is no obvious reason to suppose that these mysteries have the same source, nor, therefore, that a solution to one will solve the other.

The Global Workspace Theory

Other contemporary theorists identify consciousness with states that play a central communicative role in human cognition. The American psychologist Bernard Baars has developed a "global workspace" theory of consciousness.

Baars holds that there are a number of distinct cognitive information-processing systems in the human brain, including the various modes of perception, imagery, attention, and language. These sub-systems of the brain each have their own tasks to perform, and much of their processing takes place below the level of consciousness.

GLOBAL WORKSPACE ARCHITECTURE

These different sub-systems on occasion contribute some of their information to a "global workspace".

When they gain access to this forum, their contribution becomes available throughout the brain.

The global workspace is thus an information exchange "analogous to a blackboard in a classroom, or to a television broadcasting station" (Baars, 1988). Other sub-systems can then analyse and interpret the information from the global workspace. It is this general availability that constitutes consciousness, argues Baars.

*The information that reaches the global workspace is **conscious**, while that restricted to specialized sub-systems remains **unconscious**.*

Baars' approach happily explains the interplay of conscious and unconscious processes in perception and other mental abilities.

CAS Information-Processing

Similar theories explaining consciousness in terms of its central role in information-processing and decision-making have been developed by other psychologists. D.L. Schacter, for example, takes it that phenomenal consciousness consists of the operation of a cognitive system that mediates between "specialized knowledge modules" like vision and hearing, on the one hand, and the "executive system" controlling reasoning and action, on the other.

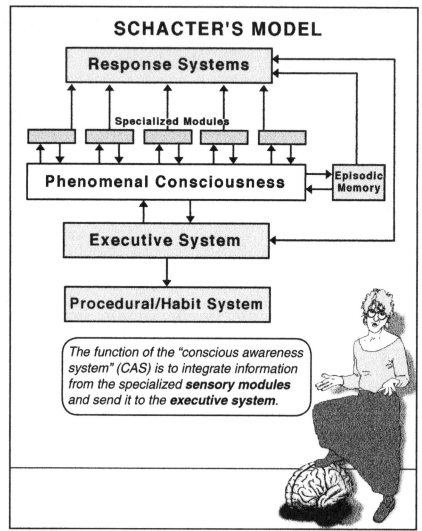

SCHACTER'S MODEL

Response Systems

Specialized Modules

Phenomenal Consciousness

Episodic Memory

Executive System

Procedural/Habit System

*The function of the "conscious awareness system" (CAS) is to integrate information from the specialized **sensory modules** and send it to the **executive system**.*

The CAS also receives information from the episodic memory store, as when we consciously recall previous experiences, and from the executive system itself, as when we are aware of our own reasoning and plans.

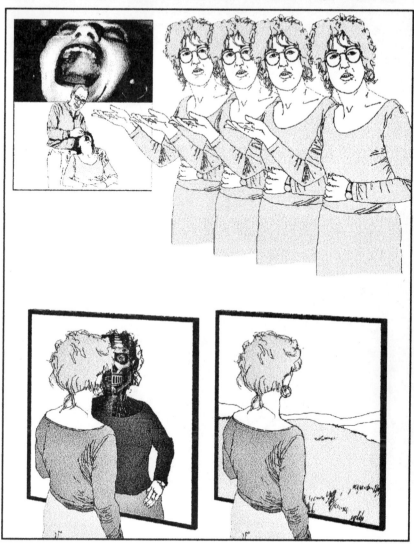

The important point, for Schacter, is that conscious information is information that subserves decisions made by the executive system, and all such information must be routed through, and integrated by, the CAS. (Note in particular how there are no arrows directly from episodic memory, or the specialized knowledge modules, to the executive system.)

Equal Rights for Extra-Terrestrials

All the theories of consciousness mentioned so far are open to an obvious objection. They all explain consciousness in **human** terms. They relate consciousness specifically to aspects of human physiology and psychology – cortical oscillations, cytoskeletal tubules, perceptual attention, language, hearing, episodic memory stores.

But it would be absurdly chauvinist to hold that only humans can be conscious.

Surely there is room for non-human consciousness?

It is one thing to hold that the feelings of other creatures, like octopuses, must be different from human feelings. We saw grounds for that much discrimination earlier.

But this is far short of saying that non-humans cannot have conscious feelings at all. Some thinkers (though not me) argue that all other **terrestrial** creatures, like cats, dogs and chimpanzees, lack consciousness.

But even if we allow this, what about possible alien life forms?

Surely intelligent extra-terrestrials could be conscious, even if constructed on radically non-human lines – without cortices, say, or hearing, or episodic memory stores. An ambitious theory of consciousness ought to cover this possibility too, and not aim only at intelligence in humans.

Intentionality and Consciousness

Perhaps we can satisfy this ambition if we explain consciousness in terms of **intentionality**. "Intentionality" is a fancy way of talking about representation. A state is intentional if it is **about** something, if it refers to something. Language is intentional in this sense.

The word "Sydney", for example, refers to a city on the other side of the world.

Many mental states share this feature of intentionality. When I **think** about Sydney (about the harbour, and the opera house, and bodysurfing on Bondi beach …), my mental state is similarly focused on the distant city.

Intentionality is a quite general, abstract property. There is no reason to think that it is peculiar to human cognition. We can expect any extra-terrestrial thought to involve intentionality too. An intentional theory of consciousness should therefore be innocent of terrestrial chauvinism.

The suggestion that the conscious mind can be explained in terms of intentionality goes back to the end of the 19th century. The German psychologist and philosopher **Franz Brentano** (1838–1917) developed the view that the essence of mentality is its directedness on objects.

All consciousness is consciousness of something.

Brentano's ideas had a great influence on another philosopher, the founder of Phenomenology, **Edmund Husserl** (1859–1938). Husserl thought that philosophy should be grounded in a careful study of the way in which consciousness presents its objects to us.

Consciousness and Representation

The equation of consciousness with intentionality is not confined to the phenomenological movement. A number of contemporary philosophers from outside that tradition have also developed representational theories of consciousness.

These include the materialists Michael Tye and Fred Dretske, as well as the dualist David Chalmers.

*Tye and Dretske want to **identify** consciousness with representation.*

Chalmers aims for a theory that will show that these are two separate but related features of mind.

*He speculates that the basic principles of his prospective science of consciousness will explain how consciousness always arises in the **presence** of representation.*

In fact Chalmers uses the technical notion of **information** rather than representation or intentionality itself. The difference is that "information" is present whenever we have sentence-like structures of elements, even if the structures are strictly meaningless.

Explaining Intentionality

Does it help to explain consciousness in terms of intentionality? Intentionality is philosophically puzzling in its own right. It may only take us deeper into philosophical quicksand.

How can words – marks on paper or patterns of sound – stand for something else, like a distant city? Well, perhaps words represent because we mentally **understand** what they mean. But this just pushes the problem back.

How does our mental **understanding** represent the distant city?

What gives our mental states the power to reach out and represent something many of us have never seen?

Given questions like these, intentionality seems as hard a problem as consciousness. So it does not seem much of a step forward to equate consciousness with intentionality.

Can We Crack Intentionality?

Aren't we just trading in one philosophical riddle for another? Not necessarily. It would be a genuine advance to show that consciousness involves nothing over and above intentionality. Where before we used to have two riddles, now we would only have one. We could stop worrying about consciousness as a separate problem and concentrate on cracking intentionality. That would be progress.

Perhaps intentionality can itself be explained. There are a few theories around which aim to solve the "hard problem" of intentionality.

These theories try to explain how intentionality fits into the objective world of causes and effects.

None of these theories is yet universally accepted, but it would be premature to conclude that no such theory can succeed. If we had a good theory of intentionality, and if consciousness were nothing more than intentionality, then we would be home free.

Non-Representational Consciousness

Still, all this assumes that consciousness **is** nothing over and above inten-tionality. But there are serious obstacles to this equation. For one thing, not all conscious states seem to be representational. In addition, not all representational states seem to be conscious.

Let us start with the first obstacle. While plenty of conscious states are intentional – like thoughts, perceptions, images and memories – as many seem not to be. For example, pains and itches.

In Defence of Representation

Defenders of the representational approach have answers. By and large, they argue that states of pain, emotion and so on, **do** have representational contents, despite first appearances to the contrary.

Even orgasms have been argued to represent physical changes in the appropriate bodily regions.

Non-Conscious Representation

The converse objection to the "consciousness = representation" equation is that plenty of representation doesn't seem to be conscious. Sentences aren't conscious, for a start, even though they represent. And what about unconscious beliefs? Their unconsciousness doesn't seem to stop them being **about things**. Here's an example.

Perhaps these are only second-hand representations, borrowing their intentionality from representations that **are** conscious. Maybe sentences only represent because they are **consciously understood** by those who use them. And maybe unconscious beliefs only represent because they are similar to **conscious beliefs** with the same content.

But there are harder cases of **non-conscious representation**.

Much cognitive processing in the brain seems to involve unconscious states that represent at first-hand, without any help from conscious ones. Within the early stages of human visual processing, for example, there are states that represent changes in the wavelength and intensity of light waves. But this is no part of conscious vision.

This kind of representation can't happily be explained as "second-hand". Nobody consciously interprets the brain states involved in visual processing, in the way people consciously interpret the sentences they speak. Nor can these states be viewed as unconscious counterparts of our conscious ones, given that most of us don't have any conscious beliefs about the properties of light waves.

Other examples of non-conscious representation can be found outside the human brain, in primitive animals and machines.

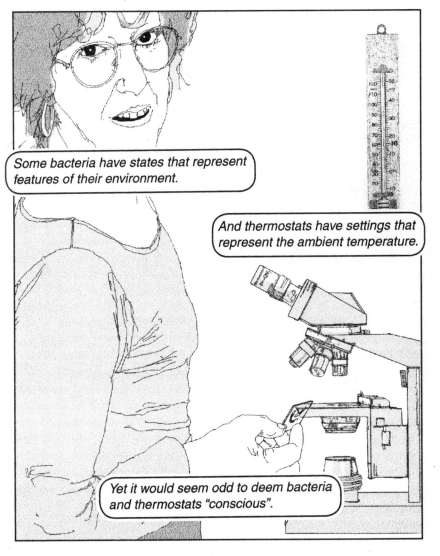

Panpsychist Representation

There are two ways for the representational approach to go here. One is to stick with the theory, and resist the intuition that there is no consciousness in bacteria, thermostats and early visual processing.

This is the option adopted by David Chalmers.

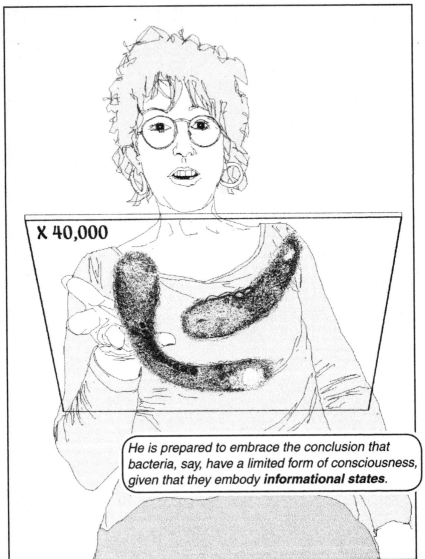

Indeed, nearly all physical systems have consciousness for Chalmers, since his definition of "information" is satisfied by pretty much any causal process. Chalmers thus ends up close to **panpsychism**.

This is the view that *consciousness pervades the natural world.*

The other option is to qualify the representational theory, and say that it is not representation as such that yields consciousness, but only representation of a **certain kind.**

Behaviour without Consciousness

A natural suggestion is that consciousness arises specifically when representations play a role in **controlling behaviour**. Michael Tye and Fred Dretske both adopt versions of this idea. This promises to deny consciousness to visual processing, bacteria and thermostats, and to any other simple systems which don't have a **range of behaviours** to control.

Unfortunately, however, behaviour-control seems insufficient to ensure consciousness.

In one classic experiment, the American physiologist Benjamin Libet asked subjects to decide spontaneously to move their hands, and simultaneously to note the precise moment of their decision, as measured by a large stopwatch on the wall.

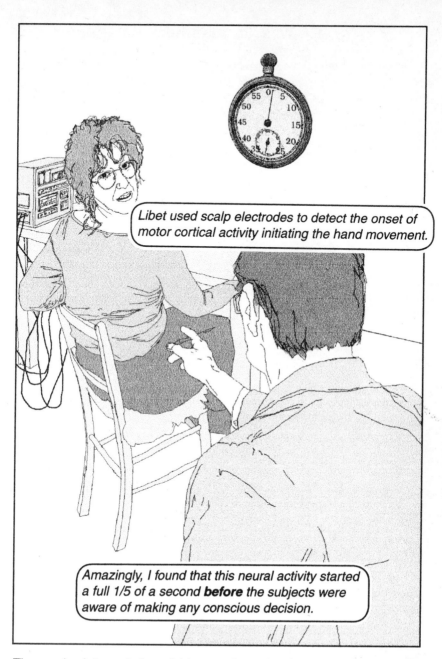

The precise interpretation of this experiment is still open to debate, but it certainly suggests that some of the processes controlling human behaviour do not involve consciousness.

What versus Where

Similar implications flow from experiments involving visual illusions. The Canadian psychologist Mel Goodale has tested subjects with arrangements of poker chips. He put one chip inside a ring of much bigger chips, and another, of the same size as the first, inside a ring of much smaller ones.

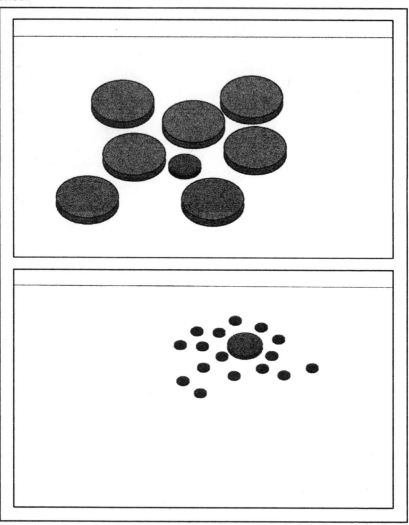

All his subjects succumbed to the conscious illusion that the first chip is much smaller than the second. But their hands weren't so easily fooled.

When they reached out to grasp the two chips, they separated their fingers by the **same amount** both times.

Here again, it seems that behaviour is controlled by non-conscious representations, rather than by conscious awareness. Many neuropsychologists now think that there are essentially two pathways in the human visual system. The "low path" leads to the conscious recognition of objects. (So it is sometimes also called the "what" path.) The "high path" contains information which controls bodily movements, like grasping with the hand. (Thus, the "where" path.) However, even though this "high path" controls behaviour, it lies below the level of consciousness.

The Problem of Blindsight

Then there is "blindsight". Some brain-damaged people can't see anything consciously. They say they are quite blind. But, even so, when they are asked to guess, they turn out to be quite good at identifying the presence of lines, flashes of light, and even colours.

To us, success at these tasks feels like unconscious guesswork.

But their ability to get the right answers shows that their performance must be controlled by genuine information which is only present at an unconscious level.

All these cases threaten the idea that representation is conscious whenever it plays a role in controlling behaviour. Perhaps this idea can be saved by clarifying what counts as "controlling behaviour". But it is not obvious how to do this, especially if we want to avoid chauvinist appeals to the details of human cognition.

HOT Theories

A different idea is that representation is only conscious when it **meta-represents** itself. Note that when we have conscious experiences, we are characteristically introspectively aware **of** those experiences. That is, we characteristically **think about** those experiences, at the same time as we are having them. This is "meta-representation".

This suggests a "higher-order thought" theory of consciousness.

This theory says that conscious mental states are precisely those mental states that we think about introspectively.

The American philosopher David Rosenthal has dubbed this the HOT theory of consciousness (**H**igher-**O**rder-**T**hought). Higher-order thinking is certainly a characteristic feature of **human** consciousness. But can a **general** theory of consciousness be built on this basis?

Criticism of HOT Theories

It seems odd to say that a state is conscious because of something that is **done** to it. Do I only become visually conscious of *Star Wars, Episode I: The Phantom Menace* when I stop thinking about Queen Amidala, and start thinking my own visual experiences instead?

If the visual experience isn't conscious in itself – when not being thought about – it's hard to see how it can be made conscious by being thought about.

In any case, HOT theories seem to demand an awful lot of sophistication in conscious creatures. They imply that beings who can't think **about** mental states can't be conscious either. This is likely to deny consciousness, not only to thermostats and bacteria, but also to rats, bats and cats.

Self-Consciousness and Theory of Mind

Creatures that can think **about** mental states are commonly said to have a "theory of mind". They are capable, not just of vision, emotion and belief, but also of forming thoughts **about** vision, emotion and belief.

Humans clearly have a "theory of mind" in this sense.

They can think about mental states, including their own.

But it is not clear that any other terrestrial animals can do this.

The classic test for having a theory of mind is the "false-belief test". Human children are able to pass this test when they are about three or four years old, though not before. Let's see how it works.

The False-Belief Test

The test hinges on this story.

Until the age of about three-and-a-half, all children say "the drawer", because they cannot handle the idea of Sally internally representing the world as other than it is.

But after four they nearly all say "the basket", because they now have the ability to attribute such a false belief to Sally.

While mature humans can all pass this test, it is not clear whether any other animals can.

At most, chimpanzees and some other apes may scrape through.

Conscious or Not?

The jury is still out on apes. Experiments have been done, mostly on chimps, but it is tricky to test chimps for a theory of mind, since they can't use words to tell you where they think Sally will look.

> *Anyway, we get bored by the experiments, and start messing around.*

In any case, even if chimps and other apes do have a theory of mind, other mammals undoubtedly don't. Cats and dogs, for example, certainly can't think about minds. This means, in particular, that they can't think about their own minds, and so, according to HOT theories of consciousness, are not conscious.

Cultural Training

Some thinkers are happy to accept the counter-intuitive conclusion that cats and dogs are not conscious. Indeed, the American philosopher Daniel Dennett is prepared to argue not only that consciousness requires something like higher-order thought, but more specifically that such thinking depends on our cultural training, and not just on our biological inheritance.

Sentience and Self-Consciousness

Most theorists reject the whole idea of consciousness as higher-order thought, and insist, in line with common sense, that many dumb animals are conscious.

It is helpful here to distinguish **self-consciousness** from **sentience**.

*Self-consciousness, understood as a matter of thinking **about** one's experiences, by definition requires higher-order thought.*

*But it seems natural to say that many animals are **sentient**, even though not self-conscious.*

Cats and dogs, for example, seem to be visually conscious of their surroundings, to hear sounds, to feel pains, and so on. These experiences are "like something" for them, even though they don't think about them.

Future Scientific Prospects

We can expect future scientific research to tell us more and more about human consciousness, as traditional investigative methods are supplemented by new brain-scanning technologies.

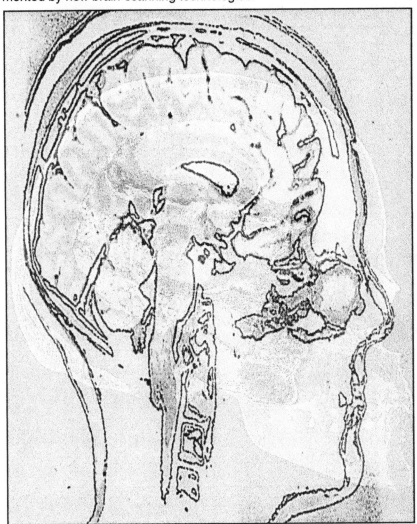

Long-standing techniques for studying human consciousness include behavioural experimentation, studies of brain damage, and electroencephalography (EEG) which measures electrical brain waves using electrodes placed in the skull.

PET and MRI

To these have recently been added Positron Emission Topography (PET) and Magnetic Resonance Imaging (MRI).

PET scans use a radioactive marker in the blood to measure brain activity. MRI scans achieve the same effect by placing the brain in a powerful magnetic field.

With the help of sophisticated computer programs, these techniques yield striking pictures of which brain areas are activated by which mental tasks. This research will give us an increasingly detailed understanding of the cerebral underpinnings of human consciousness. Whether this will lead to a **general** theory of consciousness is another matter.

The trouble is that scientific research using these techniques, or any other imaginable ones, will only tell us about consciousness in humans. This is because only humans are capable of **telling** us about their states of consciousness. People can **report** when they are conscious of seeing something and when they aren't.

Nor will it help to find out what is going on in monkey or cat brains when their (non-verbal) behaviour shows them to be sensitive to visual stimuli. For blindsight and similar phenomena show that it is quite possible to behave sensitively without consciousness.

A Signature of Consciousness

If consciousness research is lucky, it may find some suitable key feature common to all human brain states which yield consciousness. Maybe they all involve a certain kind of representation, as is claimed by intentional theories of consciousness, or maybe they all share some as-yet-unnoticed further feature.

If human consciousness research does throw up such a "signature of consciousness", then perhaps we will be able to build a general theory on this basis.

But what if there is no signature, no salient feature common to conscious human states? This seems just as likely. There may be no feature common to the states that we humans identify as conscious. Apart, that is, from their being identified as conscious, from their having the minimal common feature of introspective accessibility and reportability.

If that is all there is, then we will be stymied with non-human creatures once more.

But how then are we to decide exactly which creatures qualify for unselfconscious sentience? Cats and dogs may seem clear cases. But what about fish or crabs or snails, not to mention aliens and cybermachines? If human consciousness research doesn't turn up a clear signature, there seems nowhere else to go.

The Fly and the Fly-Bottle

Ludwig Wittgenstein thought that philosophical problems need therapy, rather than solutions, to unravel the confusions that generate them. ("We must show the fly the way out of the fly-bottle.") Perhaps this is good advice for the study of consciousness.

If we can't make progress head-on, maybe we can manoeuvre sideways, by re-examining our philosophical preconceptions.

Recall the two positive philosophical options outlined earlier, dualism and materialism. (Let us now dismiss mysterianism as unduly unambitious.)

The Dualist Option

If you are a dualist, then you won't in fact find much room for manoeuvre. For you will think that consciousness hinges on the presence of some non-physical "mind-stuff". Snails and supercomputers will be conscious just in case they have some of this special mind-stuff.

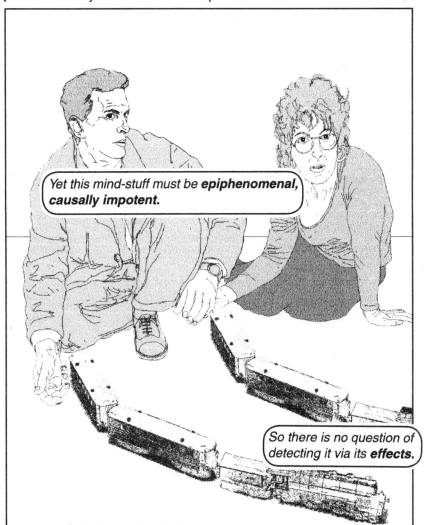

Nor does the dualist seem to have any other way of telling when it is around. Dualism thus promises to leave us eternally in the dark about the conscious life of non-human creatures.

The Materialist Option

Materialism sees things differently. There isn't any extra "mind-stuff" in humans or elsewhere. There are just physical brain processes, some of which are "like something" for the creatures that have them.

*Dualists can't help but see consciousness as a definite on-off matter – either the extra mind-stuff **is there or it isn't**.*

*But materialists have the option of viewing "what-it's-likeness" as a **continuum**.*

Some cases are pretty clear. Humans, chimps and cats are conscious. Stones, seaweed and streptococci are not. But in between there need be no fact of the matter. There need be no definite point where inner life shuts off into nothingness.

A Question of Moral Concern

Daniel Dennett has suggested that attributions of consciousness are best grounded in attitudes of moral concern. It is because we **care** about our cats that we count them as conscious.

Similarly, if we ever meet any extra-terrestrials or cyber-intelligences, it will be our mode of interaction with them that decides the issue of their consciousness.

> If we react to them as mere physical objects, then we will deem them unconscious.

> If you learn to understand and deal with such aliens, talking to us about our hopes and fears, then you will come to think of us as conscious.

No doubt some philosophical sceptics would still ask whether they are **really** conscious. But, if we make proper alien friends, this question could come to seem as silly as asking whether other human beings are really conscious.

Is There a Final Answer?

At first sight, Dennett's idea seems odd. How can a being **become** conscious just because we decide to treat it a certain way?

Of course, our embracing the aliens as objects of concern won't alter their inner life. But it might make it rational for us to define what was previously indeterminate, and extend the term "conscious" to cover that inner life.

Rather than viewing the aliens as internally uninteresting, to be lumped in with stones and streptococci, we would have found reason to classify their inner life as akin to our own.

Some of you may be disappointed to be told that there is no ultimate answer to the riddle of consciousness.

In the end, it all comes down to definitions.

But others may find satisfaction in understanding why there are no answers, and happily make your way out of the fly-bottle.

Further Reading

There are many good books on consciousness. Let me start with two useful anthologies of recent philosophical writings on the subject:

Ned Block, Owen Flanagan and Guven Guzeldere (eds.), *The Nature of Consciousness*, 1997, MIT Press.

Thomas Metzinger (ed.), *Conscious Experience*, 1996, Imprint Academic.

The next anthology has contributions from the leading scientific theorists of consciousness, including Penrose, Crick and Baars, as well as from philosophers like Dennett and Chalmers. It is a reprinting of a special multi-part issue of the *Journal of Consciousness Studies* devoted to the "hard problem".

Jonathan Shear (ed.), *Explaining Consciousness – The "Hard Problem"*, 1997, MIT Press.

Rather older, but a lot of fun, with good material on Searle's Chinese Room Argument, is this collection:

Douglas Hofstadter and Daniel Dennett (eds.), *The Mind's I*, 1985, Bantam Books.

Many of the thinkers I have discussed have written recent books:

Bernard Baars, *In the Theatre of Consciousness: The Workspace of the Mind*, 1997, Oxford University Press. Develops his "global workspace" theory of consciousness.

David Chalmers, *The Conscious Mind*, 1996, Oxford University Press. Prominent critique of materialism which has set the terms for much contemporary debate.

Francis Crick, *The Astonishing Hypothesis*, 1994, Simon and Schuster. Equates consciousness with oscillations in the visual cortex.

Daniel Dennett, *Consciousness Explained*, 1991, Allen Lane. Combines much fascinating scientific detail with the view that consciousness arrives only with human culture.

Gerald Edelman, *Brilliant Air, Brilliant Fire*, 1993, Basic Books. Explains his "neural Darwinist" view of the conscious mind.

Colin McGinn, *The Problem of Consciousness*, 1991, Basil Blackwell. Defends the "mysterian" view that the problem of consciousness lies beyond human solution.

Thomas Nagel, *The View from Nowhere*, 1986, Oxford University Press. Argues that consciousness involves a special kind of perspectival fact.

Roger Penrose, *Shadows of the Mind*, 1994, Oxford University Press. Ties consciousness to computation and quantum mechanics.

Michael Tye, *Ten Problems of Consciousness*, 1995, MIT Press. Defends a representational theory of consciousness.

Here are two useful websites for contemporary work on consciousness.

The electronic journal *Psyche*, the organ of the Association for the Scientific Study of Consciousness, is at:
http://psyche.cs.monash.edu.au/index.html
This site also hosts some discussion lists.

David Chalmers' webpage, at http://www.u.arizona.edu/~chalmers, is an excellent resource. Apart from Chalmers' own writings, it contains a substantial bibliography of work on consciousness, excellent links to other sites, and a section devoted entirely to zombies.

Biography

David Papineau was educated in Trinidad, England and South Africa. He has degrees in mathematics and philosophy, and has lectured at Reading University, Macquarie University, Sydney, Birkbeck College, London, and Cambridge University. He is now Professor of Philosophy at King's College London. He has written *For Science in the Social Sciences* (1978), *Theory and Meaning* (1979), *Reality and Representation* (1987) and *Philosophical Naturalism* (1993), and edited *Philosophy of Science* (1996). His new book, *Thinking about Consciousness*, will be published in 2001.

Index